I would like to express my deepest

Gratitude

To Dimitris, my husband and my sister Matina,
for their practical assistance and inspiration
on every step of this exciting "Odyssey".
To Stamos Triantafillou, my first mentor, and to my parents;
Nicholas Agiorgiti & Kalliroe Piperigou,
who gave me the gift of Life & Love.

November 2020

www.alkistis.net

TABLE OF CONTENTS

"Man is affected not by events,
but by the view he takes of them."

- Epictetus

Introduction

"No man can lead others, who cannot lead himself."
- Socrates

How can you lead others, if you can't even lead yourself yet ?

On the outside, you may appear strong, successful and confident. But on the inside you often feel frustrated, angry, and anxious, plagued by deep fears, that you may not even be conscious of.

According to Aristotle, one of the greatest philosophers of all time, most people have variations of these five fears:

"I'm afraid that I won't achieve anything of significance."
"I'm afraid that I'll end up all alone."
"I'm afraid that I'll get very sick."
"I'm afraid that I'm going to die."
"I'm afraid that I'll be poor."

Which one sounds most like you?

If your fear isn't listed above, take a moment to think about what it is you're most afraid of, because once you know that, you can begin to reclaim your power.

Here's an example: Years ago, during the financial crisis here in Greece, I was invited to appear on several popular TV shows to motivate and inspire the audience with my life-transforming method.

Since my first language is English, and my Greek was not very good, my first response was, "No, Thank You." Down deep inside, the truth was that I was afraid that I would make mistakes that would lead people to ridicule me.

But then, as the invitations kept coming, I thought about it a bit more, and I realized that that my fear was stopping me from connecting and making a difference.

In the end, I finally went on the shows as a guest, and I became known as "The Positive Energy Coach" (Η Προπονητρια Θετικης Ενεργειας). The result ? People would often stop me in the street to express their love and appreciation !

Alkistis appeared on popular TV shows, became known as
"The Positive Energy Coach" during the financial crisis,
inspiring and motivating millions of Greeks.

What deep desires are your fears concealing? What opportunities are you missing out on because of them?

Are you ready to gain clarity, unleash the best version of you, understand what's important and make the right decisions - the ones that will lead you to real success and happiness? If so, then you are at the right place and time to take charge of your career, your life and most importantly, *yourself.*

> *"Let he who would like to change the world,*
> *first change himself." - Socrates*

So where do you begin?

The answer has always been one - Self-Leadership.
Self-Leadership means having:

- A developed sense of *who* you are, *where* you're going, and *what* you want, as well as...
- The ability to formulate a strategy and influence and inspire yourself and others to follow it through.

Self-Leadership is probably the most important skill you can ever develop as a person and as a professional. And as you see, it's quite complicated.

The importance of self-leadership, has been taught since the beginning of history, when the ancient Greek sages recited *The Odyssey*, the story of King Odysseus setting out on a journey to return to his homeland after the end of the Trojan war. He famously faces countless dangers and hardship - monsters like the Cyclops, the Scylla and Charybdis, enchantresses like Queen Circe and the Sirens, but he never loses hope or focus, no matter how big the obstacles, because he knows what he wants. He wants to return home to his wife and family. To his kingdom. It doesn't matter that the gods, the winds and the sea are all against him. He conquers his demons, adapting to changes, keeping his course, fighting through storms and monsters, to the very end, because his goal is clear, virtuous and heartfelt, and it gives him the strength and purpose he needs.

> *"The first and greatest victory is to conquer yourself;*
> *to be conquered by yourself is of all things most*
> *shameful and vile." - Plato*

In a moment, I will reveal to you one of the most powerful methods in the world for self-leadership, based on ancient Greek philosophy.

9

But first, I would like to share some of my journey with you. I promise, I will be mercifully brief.

How I Stumbled Upon Greek Philosophy

Growing up in Canada, I was introduced to Greek philosophy by my parents, especially my father who was born a Spartan, and wanted his children to connect with their Greek heritage.

Instead of fairy tales like Cinderella and Sleeping Beauty, my father would read us bedtime stories from Aesop's Fables, The Iliad and The Odyssey.

Fast-forward to when I am about 22 years old. I am working at an international British bank in Athens. On the outside, I seem to 'have it all'; an executive position with a good salary, luxury travels and friends in 'high places'. On the inside however, I feel *frustrated and anxious* about my career path. Why? Because I've chosen banking mainly to please my father, the CEO of a major bank. I don't like it and the realization that I will have to do this for the rest of my life causes me stress and anxiety. Whenever I express my doubts about my work and my deep interest in psychology and philosophy however, my father taps me on the shoulder and says, *"My dear daughter, life is harsh and you should keep your safe, practical job no matter what...."*

Ignoring my inner truth, I stay on, feeling trapped like a hamster on a treadmill; I am unmotivated and it begins to show in a series of mistakes, arising from my negligence and lack of focus.

All these mistakes reach a climax one day; I'm called in to do an important presentation in front of the board of directors, for which I'm not sufficiently prepared. I muddle through, but in my own eyes, my performance is so bad, I am so ashamed and angry at myself, that at the end of that day, I face my deepest fears and **hand in my resignation.**

Did things get better after that? Of course not. They got much worse. I had a dramatic argument with my father, who expressed his anger, disappointment and conviction that I was making a grave mistake in letting go of a promising career. He ousted me from his house, saying what amounted to *"Tan I Epi Tas"* the ancient Spartan motto, *'Return as a victor or upon your shield'*.

Looking back at that moment though, I believe that it was *the best lesson* my father could have taught me. He cut me loose and I had to stand on my own and look at my life in harsh, unforgiving terms. I was deeply shaken, but determined to go my own way. Without a plan, I left Greece with my meager savings and backpacked through Asia Minor and Europe.

(Image: Alkistis Walking through Cappadocia, Turkey)

Soon, my money ran out and I had to find work in various low-income jobs like waitressing, temping, yoga, etc. I even tried creating my own businesses, but these ventures left me in debt.

I lived with constant fear & anxiety about money & my future. I had no purpose and no direction. It got so bad that finally, I couldn't take it any more - I decided to return home, to Greece, with my head down, face my father and ask for help and forgiveness.

Then, as I was on my way to get my return plane-ticket, I met a woman on the bus, who was working at a top leadership-training company teaching communication skills.

By a freak of luck, she was leaving her position and looking for a replacement. I told her my story and she hired me on-the-spot! It was a breakthrough for me. I loved my job, & people told me that I was very good at it.

Not only that - the founder, Dale Carnegie, was an ardent admirer of Greek philosophy. In his famous world-wide bestseller *"How To Win Friends & Influence People"*, he devotes a whole chapter to Socrates, openly admitting that he borrowed his ideas from the Master of Greek philosophy:

> ***"The ideas I stand for are not mine.***
> ***I borrowed them from Socrates…."*** *- Dale Carnegie*

I had finally found my rightful place in life. A place where I could be happy and thrive.

Now, why did I just share all of this story with you?
Because it's **a great example of what you should never do.**

I was *lucky*. Making such dramatic changes in your life without having a clue as to where you are headed and what you want, and without any proper tools to help you along the way, is foolish, ineffective and can even be down right dangerous.

It's like getting in your car without a destination or a GPS and then just driving off… A cliff, usually.

What if I told you though, that there *is* a type of GPS that can help get you to a place of thriving, happiness and freedom? A GPS inspired by the works of Socrates and Aristotle.

As mentioned above, through my work in leadership training, I was introduced to the works of the ancient Greek philosophers. They were eye-opening. One in particular stood out to me - Aristotle's timeless manual on the Art of Persuasion: *"The Rhetoric"*.

In it, Aristotle explains that there are three basic 'traits' an orator, a leader, *anyone like you and me*, must develop in order to influence and persuade others.

1. **Ethos,** which addresses the truth, credibility and integrity of the speaker.
2. **Pathos,** which addresses their emotional intelligence and use of imagination.
3. **Logos,** which addresses the logic, reason and common sense of their arguments.

Over two millennia after he wrote it, Aristotle's system is *still* the cornerstone of modern leadership skills training; His system is taught in MBA programs at top universities like Harvard, Stanford, Columbia, Yale and INSEAD. It is through Aristotle that the world's top CEOs are initiated into the **priceless 'Art of Influence and Persuasion'.**

As I taught Aristotle's method, I began to realize, there is another dimension to these 3 principles; like a treasure hidden in plain sight.

Ethos, Pathos and Logos can serve as a golden 'compass' or G.P.S. **to lead ourselves.** To help us navigate through **our own** life's endless challenges with stoic calm and certainty.

As we'll see in the next chapter, by applying them, we can attain Self-Leadership, and take charge of *ourselves* and *our* lives.

This realization that Aristotle's method for leading others could also be applied to leading one's self, transformed way of thinking. It was the tool I wish I had when I started out on my chaotic, desperate and dangerous journey. And interestingly enough, it *does* look like the "shield" my father told me to return with!

ETHOS
Your Ethical Self with Integrity, Honesty, Credibility & Good Reputation

PATHOS
Your passion & feelings, hopes & fears.

LOGOS
The logic & facts Behind your decisons.

Today, The ALKISTIS Method® seminars, trainings and e-courses are offered to both companies and the public at large, all over the world, demonstrating how these golden principles can transform frustration, anger and anxiety into calm, confident self-leadership.

I sincerely hope that you too will be inspired to become the outstanding person you are, on your journey to your homeland, *Ithaca**. (*Island-Kingdom in Homer's, *The Odyssey*)

OVERVIEW

This book is divided into 4 sections

- **The first section** of this book is an explanation of the **Core Concepts** of The ALKISTIS Method®.

- **The second section** contains the **six basic exercises** (also referred to in Greek as "Askesis") of The ALKISTIS Method®, which can empower you to gain clarity, make decisions, combat anxiety, plot your path and program your subconscious to get the results you want.

- **The third section** contains the **Philosophical Foundations**, a brief discussion of the philosophers and ideas that formed the backbone of the insights presented in The ALKISTIS Method®.

- **The fourth section** ties everything you have learned in The ALKISTIS Method® with the relevant **Scientific** discoveries and approaches of the twenty-first century.

At the end you will find useful links to life-long learning and how you can apply the method in your organization or how you can get qualified as a practitioner and trainer, so that this knowledge is spread and replicated throughout the world and benefits as many people as possible.

If you would like to find out your present competency level in Self-Leadership, take 'The Self-Leadership Quiz' at the end of this book before you proceed. This way, you can gauge your progress as you move forward.

UNITED NATIONS

"The ALKISTIS Method' resonates deeply with me... The Virtues and character traits such as Honesty, Truthfulness, Integrity, Courage and Industriousness that are enshrined in 'The ALKISTIS Method', are all familiar values which the United Nations proudly represents on a global level."

Maria - Threase Keathing, UK Country Director, **United Nations Development Programme**

SECTION 1
The ALKISTIS Method

Core Concepts

The ALKISTIS Method® is the first-ever method of self-leadership development that effectively integrates the modern scientific, evidence-based techniques of neuro-coaching, with the ageless wisdom of ancient Greek philosophy. (Especially Socrates, Plato, Aristotle and the Stoic school.)

Applied in practice, The ALKISTIS Method® leads to calm, confident, self-leadership, for both personal happiness and professional excellence, something the ancients called "*Aristeia*".

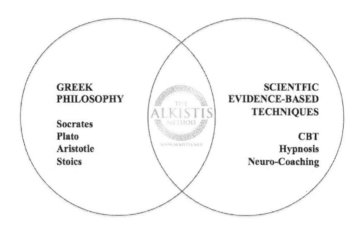

Results You Can Expect with The ALKISTIS Method®:

- Harness your greatest fears and weaknesses.
- Become an influential and effective leader.
- Embody and articulate your values, purpose and vision.
- Make positive, balanced decisions that lead to optimal results for you and your team.

- Become your most powerful self, based on your authenticity.
- Achieve authentic happiness & success.
- Manage conflict and your emotional states

Following is an overview of the core concepts. *The philosophical and scientific foundations are presented in finer detail in the third and fourth sections of this book.*

We Begin Where Aristotle Left Off...

The first book in history on the art of persuasion, *The Rhetoric*, was written by the ancient Greek philosopher Aristotle. In his book, he presents the concepts of *Ethos* (credibility), *Pathos* (emotion, imagination) and *Logos* (logic, reason), as the three traits an orator must have in order to influence and persuade his audience.

These three concepts are still the cornerstones of modern leadership today. Let us look at them in more detail:

- **Ethos** refers to the authority or credibility of the presenter; the moral values he embodies and shares with his audience. For example, being a notable figure in the field in question, or being introduced by one.

- **Pathos** refers to the audience's emotions and imagination; their hopes and fears. It can be particularly powerful if it agrees with the underlying values of the audience. Pathos also reflects the emotion or passion expressed by the speaker.

- **Logos** refers to the facts, data and evidence presented to support the claims, thesis or position of the speaker. The word *"logic"* is derived from the Greek word, *Logos*.

This is the basic diagram showing Aristotle's system "The Rhetorical Triangle", as it is known:

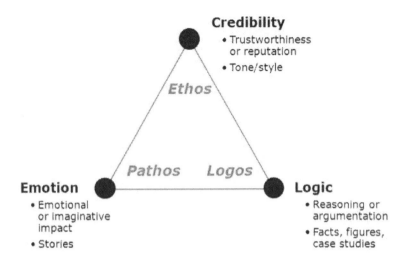

Additionally, there are two more, lesser known traits identified by Aristotle - *Telos* and *Kairos*. **Telos** (end / destination / outcome), addresses the end-goal, purpose or attitude of a speech, and **Kairos** (timing), addresses the particular setting, context, atmosphere, time, and place that a speech occurs in. We will not consider these separately, but rather include them in **Logos**, as they address the real, 'logical' considerations we must take into account to make our campaign a success.

For Aristotle, Ethos, Pathos and Logos, address the qualities that transform an ordinary person *into a great influencer, someone who can inspire and lead others.*

The unique approach of The ALKISTIS Method® is that these same traits are applied to *oneself.*

You will become the outstanding leader and influencer and you will apply these insights to lead *yourself*, to take charge of your life and guide yourself to fulfillment.

The ALKISTIS Method® refocuses Aristotle's insights and broadens their scope. It includes such things as making well thought out, balanced decisions and mastering your thoughts and emotions to command your psycho - physiological 'state'.

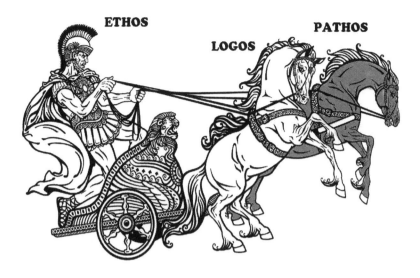

ETHOS   LOGOS   PATHOS

The Charioteer of The ALKISTIS Method®

To better visualize the core concepts of Self Leadership as set out in The ALKISTIS Method®, we will borrow the metaphor of the Charioteer, from Plato's famous book *Phaedrus*. Hereunder is the adaptation of this concept. The original version is described in Section 3 of this book, under "Plato".

The Essence of Self-Leadership is to harness the power of your mind (and body), like a charioteer harnesses horses.

Imagine then a **charioteer** (*Ethos*), in charge of navigating us to a specific compelling end, outcome or destination. The charioteer may have to take turns, go through many intermediate destinations, but his end goal is always to reach the state of **Eudaimonia**, a state where we are at our happiest, most fulfilled and most productive.

He is harnessing two majestic stallions, one black, the other white.

The **horses** represent the 'battle in the human mind'; a battle that revolves around impulse control. A tug-of-war between your emotions, hopes, desires and fears (*Pathos*), and a logical, strategic, moderating counterforce (*Logos*). *Logos and Pathos*, need to stay balanced and 'in sync', throughout the journey. They must work together and gallop in stride, led by the charioteer's firm, confident

21

hand. Harnessing these opposing forces, and driving them in alignment with your Ethos, is crucial for anyone trying to take charge of their lives, whether it's a leader, a CEO or anyone else. Being too uninformed, too impulsive, too hesitant, or not true to yourself, can spell trouble at work and in your private life.

The 3 Principles as embodied in the Charioteer Allegory

- The **Charioteer**, represents '**Ethos**'; our true, authentic self, or as Plato has it, our "Soul". Ideally, this "True Self" has integrity, honesty and ethos, but most of all, wants what's best for us, to guide us to the state of Eudaimonia.

- **The Black Horse,** is about addressing our '**Pathos**'; our emotions, motivation, hopes, desires and dreams. Also our deepest fears and weaknesses.

- The **White Horse**, is about addressing '**Logos**', or logic; the part that examines and calculates. The 'reality-check' part, that makes sure our hopes and fears are based on practical thinking, strategy, numbers and reason.

The above principles or traits provide structure - a way of organizing your internal world so that you have more control over what your brain does. It aims to reprogram your neuropsychology for success on all levels - beyond just positive thinking or affirmations.

> *"We cannot choose our external circumstances, but we*
> *can always choose how we will respond to them."*
> *- Epictetus*

It's essential that you have more control over how you feel, and what you do, because if you change the way you think, it changes the way you feel, which changes the way you act, giving you better, longer lasting results.

As mentioned above, all our efforts are directed towards reaching the state of *Eudaimonia,* - a Greek word encapsulating the notions of success, happiness and prosperity, (ie "human flourishing"). This is our real ultimate goal. *In this, Ethos, Pathos and Logos function together like a GPS, an inner compass, to help us navigate our way with confidence and efficiency.*

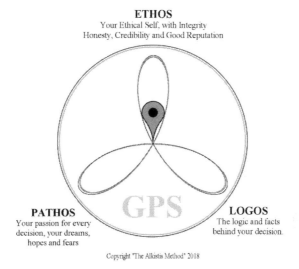

ETHOS
Your Ethical Self, with Integrity
Honesty, Credibility and Good Reputation

GPS

PATHOS
Your passion for every
decision, your dreams,
hopes and fears

LOGOS
The logic and facts
behind your decision.

Copyright "The Alkistis Method" 2018

The path to *Eudaimonia* requires that we face reality, accept the present moment as it presents itself, not allowing ourselves to be controlled by our desire for pleasure or our fear of pain.

We will examine these in more detail, but as an example, let's take a moment to see how I could have applied these concepts to my own situation which I described in the introduction.

First, I would have examined my Ethos:

Did I have integrity as the charioteer should? Was I being fair and truthful to myself? To my father? To my employers? The answer would have been a resounding "No". I am, by nature, a "people" person, not a "numbers" person and could never be happy (and therefore successful) in the job that I had. I wasn't being fair to anyone, most of all myself.

That stark realization would have led me to the conclusion that I *had* to change. That if I did not change, I would never reach eudaimonia.

Next, I would have examined my Pathos.

What did I love most? What did I fear most? What did I really want to do with my life? The answers were there. I wanted to be with people. I loved psychology, philosophy and social interaction.

Then I would have examined my Logos.

What kind of job would suit me? What did I fear? What did I hope for? Were my fears correct, or overblown? Were my hopes based on reality? Could I create a strategy to make a smoother transition into my new career? I could have even steered my job within the bank toward something relevant, such as training or human resources, which would have gained me more experience with what I loved most.

It doesn't mean that I wouldn't have faced problems. Change is always difficult and dangerous and sometimes circumstances may not even allow it. But I would know what I wanted and have a rough plan for achieving it as well as the knowledge that I was doing the right thing. I would have avoided a lot of the stress and anxiety that I had to go through and reached my goals quicker, without all the drama and uncertainty.

The 3 Golden Principles in More Detail

Ethos - The Leader's Edge

Let's face it, in real life, leaders are not always virtuous or ethical. Take Hitler and Stalin, as extreme examples. They had a great number of followers and were very powerful leaders. They were not, however, *good* leaders. They ultimately led their followers to death and destruction because their vision was flawed and their tactics lacked virtue or integrity. This fact becomes very important when it comes to leading *yourself*. You *must* be true and virtuous then, otherwise you'll be leading *yourself* astray. Deep happiness and fulfillment (*Eudaimonia*), according to the Greek philosophers, can never be attained by a malicious character.

In order to become a good and effective leader of yourself, brutally honest self-inquiry and self-regulation are paramount. They are essential skills. As Shakespeare wrote in Hamlet: *To thy own self be true.* You must understand yourself, who you are at your core, and figure out what is best for **your wellbeing** and the inner "tribe" you are leading. You must set compelling goals, and create a vision that will inspire **the whole of you**. This, according to the Greek philosophers, is the way to 'attract' your state of *Eudaimonia*. Your promised land. Your *'Ithaca'*. *Ithaca (Island-Kingdom in the Odyssey)

"He who cannot lead himself, cannot lead others."
- Socrates

There are many ego-traps you can fall into when considering this. You may think, for example, that the goal of your life is to earn as much money as possible, and that *virtue* and all those other lofty ideals should be followed by *others,* and not by you - as long as you can get away with it.

Socrates however, would tell you that you are on the wrong path; that **moral virtue (*Areté*) is the greatest good in life**, because it alone is capable of securing one's authentic happiness and fulfillment. He advises us not to try to deceive others, even if we could get away with it:

"Be as you wish to seem" - Socrates

Ethos, he teaches, is not just something you wear for the outside world. It is something you *practice* and *embody* everyday in your life, because even if no one is watching, you yourself will know.

Now, you may be thinking that this is too idealistic; too naive...

Consider though that honesty, virtue and morality are more than just religious or philosophical ideals. They are *instincts* deeply embedded in our DNA. They don't only benefit us as individuals, protecting us from the deceit and abuse of others, they also benefit our societies. We are all the descendants of people who managed to collaborate and live in groups strong enough to persist through invasions and natural disasters. In order to survive, progress and thrive, our forefathers had to be in some way *loyal to each other*, display *empathy, respect, cooperation and 'obey common laws'* to empower their groups and keep them strong, cohesive and productive. They had to be and do all the things we today *instinctively* consider as *"good"*.

These codes of behaviour, have evolved into our values, the values of the Civilized World. Our basic values have held our relationships, families and communities together throughout our history. If we cheat, we undermine them, we sabotage ourselves and civilization itself, and knowing this, deep inside, we can never be *truly* happy and fulfilled.

Think of it this way - we all *want* to **live in a better, safer and more civilized society**. We therefore *want* virtue and values to exist.

We also want to be considered a **valued member** of that society. We seek the true love, trust, respect and acceptance of others. It empowers us. We don't want to be seen as liars, con-men and cheats. Those, we persecute through our justice system. We shun and punish them.

It follows then, that if we want to be happy, **we *must* behave with Ethos, because if we don't, we become the very thing we despise**. Even if no one else knows, *we* know, and we become inwardly un-aligned. The person we display to the world is not the person we really are. It's a conflict that breeds inside us, resulting in misery and *'dis-ease'*. It's not the path to *Excellence* or *Eudaimonia*.

This means that having **Ethos is not idealistic or naive, but is in fact the *most selfish thing we can do*,** since we are catering to *our own* happiness, without taking anyone or anything else into account. Ethos is its own reward.

Ethos will also benefit you on a purely utilitarian level.

First of all, living with Ethos will gain you a good **reputation**. It will make you more *trustworthy*, a priceless commodity in business and personal relations. Ask yourself - who would you rather employ or be employed by? Who would you want as a friend? A partner? Being perceived as trustworthy is like being given the keys to a door.

Ethos will create a healthier overall environment wherever it's applied; a beneficial rising tide that sweeps through our society, lifting everyone up.

Ask yourself this - what type of country would you like to live in? More importantly, what type of country would you *invest your money* in? The answer is simple. A country you *trust*. A country whose institutions work well and where you can be sure you will be treated with fairness and justice. In short, *a country with Ethos*. This bears out in reality. Countries with ethos; with justice and fair, independent institutions, have, all things being equal, done much better than countries without them, to the benefit and prosperity of everyone living there.

It's why all leaders, governments and political systems claim (even if falsely) to have it. We know instinctively that it benefits everyone, from our families to our communities, businesses, institutions and governments.

Second, Ethos will give you **strength** and purpose, because it will give you the **freedom to be who you are**. Your thoughts, beliefs and actions will all be aligned, giving you strength and confidence because you know you're doing the right thing. It's like a shield you can wear to fend off fear and doubt.

It's why all ideologies and religions in the world embrace and require it. It is the central idea behind their teachings and aimed at your personal well-being as well as that of the society in which you live.

Virtue (Greek: *Areté*), the cornerstone of Ethos, *is not therefore an abstract term* for philosophy, but a very concrete aspect of our personal *happiness, freedom and fulfillmen*t. **We should be ethical, not only because it's the 'right thing' to do, but for purely selfish reasons.** It benefits *us* and *our* well being.

As Marcus Aurelius, Roman Emperor and devout student of Greek philosophy wrote 2,000 years ago:

"No matter what anyone says or does, my task is to be good. Like gold or emerald or purple repeating to itself, 'No matter what anyone says or does, my task is to be emerald, my color undiminished.'"

Ethos, therefore, should be the first filter any decision we make needs to pass through. It is our character - our only true possession.

We don't have to be perfect. No one is. Life is complicated and difficult. But we must strive to be as *excellent* as possible.

Let us start by asking ourselves the fundamental questions that will help us clarify the values that we choose to live by. Questions that any self-respecting person and professional needs to address to command respect and influence others:

- What are the core values I wish to live by?
- What matters most to me?
- What is my Life Purpose ?
- What legacy do I want to leave behind?

The ALKISTIS Method® recommends adopting *the four cardinal virtues* in defining your Ethos because practicing these will inevitably lead to your fulfillment and Eudaimonia.

The Four Cardinal Virtues: Wisdom (Greek phronêsis), **Justice** (Greek dikaiosunê), **Courage** (Greek andreia), **Temperance** (Greek sôphrosunê)

Historians can't agree on where this classification originated. It appears to go back as far as Plato or Socrates, although some argue that they can be traced back to about the 12th-8th centuries B.C., to Homer's epic poems, *The Iliad* and *The Odyssey*.

Wisdom *(phronêsis)*

This is the common sense ability to know good from bad. We apply wisdom to judge what is to be done and what is not to be done and to know what is under our control and what is not.

Includes good calculation, quick-wittedness, cunning, discretion, and resourcefulness.

Justice *(dikaiosunê)*

To be fair and just in our *treatment of others*. To be moral, honest, and conduct ourselves with the dignity, equity, and fairness, we demand of others.

Courage *(andreia)*

To resist fear; to be courageous without being reckless. To have confidence and self-restraint about what is truly fearful and terrible; to be bold wisely; intrepid in the face of hardship and death. Includes discipline, confidence, and self-control.

Temperance *(sôphrosunê)*

Moderation concerning desires and pleasures; harmony and good discipline. It has to do with personal independence, and self -discipline; rational acceptance of what is admirable and contemptible. Includes endurance, modesty, high-mindedness, cheerfulness, and industriousness.

These virtues derive initially from Plato's Republic Book IV, 426–435. The Roman Emperor Marcus Aurelius discusses them in Book V:12 of Meditations and views them as the "goods" that a person should identify in one's own mind, as opposed to "wealth or things which conduce to luxury or prestige." These cardinal virtues are listed in the Bible, as they were adopted by early Christians, who added on the three theological virtues of faith, hope and charity.

The cardinal virtues are considered the 'antidote' to the capital vices of *pride, greed, lust, envy, gluttony, wrath and sloth*. If you build your life and ambitions around these vices, you will probably be disappointed, because the pleasure they offer is *ephemeral*. It doesn't mean that we don't seek and enjoy pleasurable things like acclaim and monetary success. It means that we don't "require" them to be happy and fulfilled; to "flourish" in a state of *Eudaimonia*.

To clarify your personal Ethos, Stephen Covey, author of *"The 7 Habits of Highly Successful People"*, recommends writing a 'Personal Mission Statement':

> *"Writing or reviewing a mission statement changes you because it forces you to think through your priorities deeply, carefully, and to align your behaviour with your beliefs".*

We apply all this in Section 2, The Askesis (exercises). Most professionals are very familiar with their company's mission statement, but few have clearly formulated one for themselves.

Words to live by

Some other words that embody ideas which have endured in philosophy because great minds have found them to be valid and wise, are:

Prosoche - (Gr. προσοχή, attention, focus) - Your brain runs all the time, and it's either going to run in the direction *you* want it to go, or it's going to run *all over the place*. If you don't *take charge* of your thoughts and manage what images you are forming, then you won't be performing at your peak, or getting the results that you really want. *That is why it's important to observe, organize and manage your thoughts and energy,* a process the ancient Greeks called *'Prosoche'*. (Discussed in more detail later on).

Ataraxia - (Gr. ἀταραξία,, generally translated as "equanimity", or "tranquillity") - is a Greek philosophical term for a lucid state of robust equanimity that is characterized by ongoing freedom from distress and worry on a deep level. Not to be confused with indifference or carelessness, it means fully taking charge of oneself and the situation at hand by being calm and collected.

Pathos & Logos - Your Two Powerful Stallions

Pathos and Logos should be considered together. Ultimately, they serve the same purpose - to pull the chariot that the Charioteer (Ethos) commands, towards *Eudaimonia* (happiness, success and fulfillment). They can be described in the following way:

Pathos- Your Black Stallion

Pathos is your *passion*; your ability to harness and channel your emotional states to influence and appeal to the emotions of your team or 'audience'. Aristotle addressed Pathos as a vital part of the art of persuasion ie awakening emotion in the audience so as to influence them to reach the desired conclusions and actions.

In The ALKISTIS Method®, the 'audience' is *yourself*. Your Pathos is directed towards *you*. You must search within yourself to find what motivates and inspires you and channel your emotions appropriately. It is how you fan your ambition, become inspired, activate your courage and resilience to carry you forward and overcome your fears, anxieties and doubts.

Examining your emotions will furnish you with vital information about who you are and what you really want i.e. your deep desires. It will clarify your goals and reveal subconscious fears and hopes that may be very important to consider. The ability to align yourself correctly with what you feel most strongly about makes everything else easier and more naturally flowing.

Understanding your own Pathos will also help you understand, harmonize and harness the power of *other* people's hopes and emotions. This is a very powerful ability that will greatly increase your chances of achieving your goals by persuading others to see your point of view and join your vision. Feeling the passion within yourself is a direct path to reaching other people's hearts.

Logos- Your White Stallion

Logos is your ability to apply logical, objective, realistic and strategic thinking for influencing yourself and others. It's the *proof* behind your theories; the evidence you need to supply your audience with, to convince them that you're not just a daydreamer or a wishful thinker, but that your proposals are rational and feasible. To do this, you need to understand the subject well, thoroughly processing it through your Logos. Only then will you be able to successfully communicate it to others.

This is even more important when *you are leading yourself.* You want the best for you. Be vigilant. Review your first impressions. Test your conclusions. How true are the 'facts' behind them?

Applying Logos and Pathos, in alignment with our Ethos, is what The Alkistis Method® is about. For a more detailed look at how this can be achieved, refer to Section 2, The Askesis (exercises)

Interestingly, neuroscience has found that there is a division of some of our mind's functionality, reminiscent of Logos and Pathos, between the right and left hemispheres of our brains. Even modern psychology, speaks of "IQ" (Intelligence quotient) and "E.Q." (Emotional Quotient), concepts similar to those deduced by Aristotle over two millennia ago.

Using Ethos, Pathos, Logos to understand others

Lastly, these three traits Aristotle identified, can also help you better understand *other* people. It is difficult sometimes to gauge the intentions and substance of someone you just met, and examining each of these traits separately can give you better insight. Ask yourself: What is their *Ethos*? Their history, their reputation? Do they have integrity? What is their *Pathos*? Their motivation, their hopes and fears. What is their *Logos*? Are their facts correct? Are they reasonable? It is certainly not a full proof method, but it will offer your a well-founded first impression.

The Desire of Knowledge

In an anecdotal story from ancient Greece, Socrates, widely accepted as the wisest person of his time, was walking down a sandy shore with Plato, his pupil, a young man from a prominent family who passionately desired to learn from the master.

At one point, Socrates said to Plato, *"Walk with me into the sea."*

As they ventured in and the water started to slowly rise above their ankles, then their knees, Plato wondered, *"What is the lesson my master is trying to teach me?"* When the water reached to shoulder height, Socrates abruptly grabbed Plato's head and pushed him down under the water. Plato didn't react in the beginning, thinking it was an exercise of some sort, but soon, as he started running out of oxygen, he began to struggle and fight back. Socrates however, a builder by trade and strong despite his age, held him down until Plato could take no more and had to seriously fight for his life to free himself from his mentor's relentless grasp.

When he regained his breath, he angrily accused Socrates of trying to drown him.

Socrates replied calmly: *"That was not my intention of course. What I showed you, is what it takes to gain true knowledge and wisdom.*

When you desire it like you desired that breath of air, then you shall have it."

Similarly, you must ask yourself, *how badly do you want the inner freedom and other benefits of Self Leadership?* Are you willing to follow through with the rigorous training - the *Askesis*? Are you ready to leave your comfort zone?

You must want the benefits of proper Self Leadership as much as 'a drowning person wants oxygen', to reap its full benefits.

As an inspiration, it may help you to gaze into the eyes of one of the most beautiful and famous statues of the ancient world, *The Charioteer of Delphi.*

Image: Photo taken at National Archeological Museum of Delphi

35

The Charioteer is not portraying the struggle *during* the race, but an enchanted state, right after he has won the race, as he takes the victory-lap around the stadium to the sound of a cheering crowd.

His mesmerizing gemstone eyes evoke what the Greeks of the Classical period referred to as *Areté* (virtue, moral excellence, true nobility).

Despite his great victory, there are no shouts or wild celebration, only contentment and calm inner strength. The face and body do not convey arrogance, only the sense of deep, serene self confidence and satisfaction. He did not succeed through luck or divine providence. He succeeded through clarity of purpose, hard work, and virtue. He deserves his place at the podium.

*Suggested: Before going on to the next section, ponder on the above, while listening to the inspirational, epic musical piece **Chariots of Fire**. (Composed by contemporary Greek composer Vangelis.) Then, write down your thoughts in a journal.*

SECTION 2
The Askesis

Exercises for Self-leadership

Exercises for Self-leadership

Over the past twenty years, as an executive consultant and coach for dozens of the world's largest and most progressive companies, I've experienced my clients spending millions with top consulting firms to implement change management or leadership development initiatives. Many months later, these consulting firms invariably delivered comprehensive and detailed 'Lean and Six Sigma' roadmaps to a future that *looked great in their reports*. That was the *easy* part. The hard part, which was not always successful, was inspiring individuals on each functional team to *willingly* take action.

That's where **The ALKISTIS Method®** offers help, to make change happen in practice. Its success lies in its application - not its reports.

Applying The ALKISTIS Method®

As you have already realized by now, the concepts of The ALKISTIS Method® *can only be assimilated and understood through experience* and practice, which is **not** the same thing as knowing them *intellectually*. (Imagine the difference between swimming in the sea, and thinking about swimming in the sea.)

Daily practice requires personal 'Work' on observing the flow of your thoughts, honest self-reflection, and a flexible mindset capable of making leaps, but also exercising temperance.

"Don't explain your philosophy. Embody it." - Epictetus

American philosopher Henry David Thoreau conveyed the problem of modern western philosophy in his book *Walden, Life in the Woods*.

> *"There are nowadays professors of philosophy, but not philosophers. To be a philosopher is not merely to have subtle thoughts, [. . .] but to so love wisdom as to live according to its dictates, a life of simplicity, independence,*

magnanimity, and trust. It is to solve some of the problems of life, not only theoretically, but practically.

In other words, modern philosophy has become *a discourse about* philosophy.

Philosophy is a practice not a theory. Unlike modern academia, philosophy was, first and foremost, about learning **how to live well** - not only thinking about it.

A philosophy school in the Golden Age of Greece was meant to *transform the lives of its students*; To break their chains and realize their potential. (See Plato's Allegory of The Cave later on.) The same applies to Self Leadership. It's all about applying oneself on all levels. The insights philosophy gives are viewed as a way of life and become our daily *practice towards personal awakening and excellence.*

In the Greek language, the practice and application of what one 'knows' is called *'Askesis'*, and it is the key to personal awakening. *Askesis (pronounced ask-ee-sis) means:* rigorous 'training', 'practicing' and 'self-discipline' from Greek *askein* 'to exercise'. Hence an *'ascetic' is someone who 'practices', a practitioner towards improving and mastering one's physical, emotional and mental abilities.*

The *Askesis* here, are based on a neuro-coaching approach which is scientifically tested and highly effective. In combination with concepts from Greek philosophy, they represent an integration of applied neuroscience, performance psychology and neurolinguistics.

In these Askesis, the *emphasis* is on neurology and engaging *the whole nervous system,* all three of our 'brains', the spinal cord and peripheral nerves for high performance and wellbeing. This differs from other forms of coaching and training methods because we are retaining *the central importance* of using neurological or 'embodied thinking' processes, rather than relying on advice-style models of coaching. The benefits and potential of neurocoaching cannot be overstated.

It has been scientifically proven that when we read something or hear it, we retain only a 10-20% of the knowledge, whereas, when we participate with our whole nervous system in various exercises, we retain up to 100 %, even after several years have passed.

The idea that the way we think can *physically alter our brain* at the neural-level and reverse previous learning, impairment or damage, is central to neuro-coaching. *Scientific studies in psycho-cybernetics have shown that it takes as little as sixty-six days to take on a new habit.*

Many Askesis are based on the most recent research we have on the human brain and how it affects our physical, emotional and mental states. That's why they are often accompanied by music, visual-arts and specific physical movements in the seminars and workshops.

The Askesis cultivate **Prosochē** (attention, focus - discussed at the end of the section on Ethos, "Words to live by").

> *When you relax your attention for a while, do not fancy*
> *you will recover it whenever you please, but remember*
> *this, that because of your fault of today your affairs must*
> *necessarily be in a worse condition in future occasions.*
> *-Epictetus (Discourses 4.12.1)*

In time, as you develop and deepen the attitude and practice of *prosochē,* you will become a *prokoptōn* (one who is making progress). The practice of self-observation, does not demand perfection. It demands that one does it. Prosoche requires attention and focus. The goal of the *prokoptōn* is continual progress - "Ever to excel" (Greek: "Αιέν αριστεύειν")

The upcoming Askesis of The ALKISTIS Method® not only develop your *prosoche* but also give you a very good basis, from which to filter your experience and observations. On the path to

Eudaimonia, you need to know who you are, what you want and where you want to go.

The 6 major Askesis of The ALKISTIS Method®

I.   THE CHARIOTEER'S CHOICE®
     Make Well, Thought-Out , Balanced Decisions

II. THE SOCRATIC TEST®
     Master Your Thoughts & Emotions

III. DEFINE YOUR ITHACA®
     Formulate Your Personal Mission Statement

IV. MORPHEAS MIND MECHANICS®
     Program Your Subconscious For Success (mp3)

V.   THE MAP OF ULYSSES®
     Create a Future Vision of your Life

VI. MASTER OF RHETORIC®
     Influence Others With Ease

A full explanation of these Askesis with video-tutorials is available through The ALKISTIS Method® E-Learning Program:
www.alkistis.net/e_learning.html

Askesis I - THE CHARIOTEER'S CHOICE®
Make Well, Thought-Out, Balanced Decisions

Background:

Making decisions can, in most cases, be hard, because there are many factors and risks involved. The most important thing though, is that you *make them*. Neuroscience tells us that *reaching decisions reduces your worry and anxiety and helps you solve problems, even if the decision you reach is only "good enough"*.

You can never have *all* the information, so you can never reach the perfect decision. It will always have a degree of uncertainty. The point is that the more you exercise your Ethos, Pathos and Logos 'muscles', the better your decision-making will be, the less the uncertainty you will face and the happier you will feel about it. So much time and energy is lost, when we are unclear, undecided or we procrastinate.

"While we wait for life, life passes" -**Seneca**

In his presentation of the concepts of Ethos, Pathos and Logos, Aristotle was referring to the traits an orator must have in order to influence and persuade his audience. Also, as mentioned earlier on in this book, there are two other, lesser known principles that Aristotle identified, that of **Telos** (end, goal, completion) and **Kairos** (timing, context). For simplicity, we generally consider these to be included in the **Logos** trait, since they address logical, strategic matters.

Together, these traits represent *the most basic questions* we can ask regarding *any* situation or problem we are faced with i.e. *Who, Why, What, Where* and *When*:

- **Ethos** addresses **Who** you are.

- **Pathos** addresses **Why** you want what you want.

- **Logos** addresses **What** and **How**; your actual strategy and the realities you are facing.

- **Telos** addresses **Where**; as in where you want to go - the actual outcome you seek to achieve.

- **Kairos** addresses **When**; the best time to act/ your timing.

Together, these force you to examine the full spectrum of considerations which you must address in order to reach a balanced decision for yourself (or to persuade others that your decision is valid.)

It's like calibrating the G.P.S. of your mind with a clear address, allowing you to achieve your goals in the most ideal way. It's a process of checks and balances. and working to gain the knowledge, courage and confidence needed to set correct goals and take the most beneficial, balanced and informed decisions possible.

NOTE: This Askesis is best done after you have completed the Askesis DEFINE YOUR ITHACA® and THE MAP OF ULYSSES®

Name: THE CHARIOTEER'S CHOICE®

Purpose: To help you to think more clearly and arrive at the best decision possible, through processing your thoughts and feelings.

Instructions:

 Briefly describe the dilemma or issue that you are facing and which requires a decision to be made.

 What are the 2-3 possible solutions/options/paths according to your understanding of the situation?

You will then proceed to pass through the first filters of Ethos, Pathos, Logos.

"The Three Filters"

1. **Ethos Filter** - Be honest and truthful with yourself. Is the path or solution that you are thinking about, aligned with who you are? Is it aligned with your integrity, your character, your core values and your best interests? Does it reflect who you aspire to be; your authentic, "Best Self"? Is it aligned with your purpose in life, and the future vision you have for yourself? (See later on the askesis on creating your Personal Mission Statement)

 Write down your thoughts...

2. **Pathos Filter** - Consider Pathos - your emotions, hopes, desires and dreams as well as fears. How do you *feel* about it? What does your gut say? What emotions does it evoke in you? Emotions express your subconscious thinking and will usually reveal actual problems or opportunities. Pathos will compel you on the one hand, raising your hopes that your dreams can be achieved, but on the other hand, it may paralyze you with fear and self-doubt, making you waver with indecision. Answer these questions:

 What is your BIG WHY - your deeply emotional reason for doing this?
What is holding you back?
Write about your 3 Fears/Main Concerns.

3. **Logos Filter - What** and **How**. Logos is your reality-check. Consider the hopes and fears you listed above in view of the actual realities you are facing. Looking at the facts, are your fears overblown or are your hopes too naive and optimistic?

The only way to know is *to work the numbers and list the facts.* What do they say? What does 'common sense' say? What are the logical, rational steps and strategies that must be followed? What proofs, evidence, examples or case-studies do you have?

What is the 'usefulness' of this path you are choosing? Does it serve the general plan of your life?

Telos: What is your exact goal and is it beneficial to you in the short term as well as in the long term?

Kairos: Is this the right time?

*Note: It is always a good idea to discuss your thoughts with a **mentor**, coach or consultant, to get someone else's point of view. Explaining your thought process to someone else, getting their feedback and answering their questions will open your eyes to matters you may not have considered.*

 Finally, take a decision and write it down.

Askesis II - THE SOCRATIC TEST®
Master Your Thoughts & Emotions

Background: Managing your *psycho-physiological state is no easy task*, especially when there are deep seated fears and insecurities, that flare up when triggered by some external event. The application of a 'filtering system', representative of Ethos, Pathos and Logos, for dealing with unwanted, disturbing thoughts, is very useful, as this anecdotal story with Socrates demonstrates.

A long time ago in ancient Athens, the great philosopher is said to have come upon an acquaintance, who ran up to him excitedly and said, *"Socrates, do you know what I just heard about one of your students?"*

"Wait a moment," Socrates replied. *"Before you tell me, I'd like you to pass a little test. It's called the Test of Three."*

"Test of Three?"

"Yes," Socrates continued. *"Before you talk to me about my student let's take a moment to test what you're going to say. The first test is* ***Truth***. *Have you made absolutely sure that what you are about to tell me is true?"*

"*No.*" the man replied, "*Actually I just heard about it.*"

"*All right,*" said Socrates. "*So you don't really know if it's true or not. Now let's try the second test, the test of **Kindness**. Is what you are about to tell me about my student something good?*"

"*No, on the contrary...*"

"*So,*" Socrates continued, "*you want to tell me something bad about him, even though you're not certain it's true?*"

The man shrugged, a little embarrassed.

Socrates continued, "*You may still pass though because there is a third test – the test of **Usefulness**. Is what you want to tell me about my student going to be useful to me?*"

"*No, not really...*"

"Well." concluded Socrates, "If what you want to tell me, is neither true nor good nor even useful, then why tell it to me at all?"

As this story reveals, there are three filters we must pass our thoughts and beliefs through before allowing them to dwell in our minds:

1. **Is it True?**
    Represents **Ethos** (Consider: Integrity, Credibility, Accuracy)

2. **Is it Kind?**
    Represents **Pathos** (Consider: Feelings, Emotions, Compassion, Kindness, Empathy)

3. **Is it Useful?**
    Represents **Logos** (Consider: Reason, Practicality, Applicability, Utility, Facts, Strategies)

Now try it for yourself:

Name: "THE SOCRATIC TEST"®

Purpose: Using three 'filters' to overcome distressing, frustrating, angering, fear-filled thoughts and beliefs you may presently hold, and keep your mind lean and efficient.

Instructions: Bring to mind a particular thought or belief that worries, distresses or angers you, regarding your personal or professional life. It can be a large or small thing.

The best way to do this is to 'visit the scene' as if you are watching it on a TV screen:

If the frustrating, angering or frightening event happened in the past, revisit and relive the scene to review it and connect with your fear. For example:

The year is 1989. I'm in the living room of my parents' home. I'm having (the usual) argument with my father... about me wanting to leave my job at the bank.

The belief that worries, stresses, frustrated me down deep inside:

"If I ever leave my job, he'll be so disappointed in me. I'll lose his love and admiration. He won't forgive me."

And what does that mean about me?
"It means that I'm not worthy."
- That's the (false) belief that I'm holding about myself.

Now it's your turn; prepare yourself to write down the exact frustrating, angering or frightening thought or belief (in one or two sentences), exactly as it is formulated when you think it. It's a belief that you presently hold about yourself, another person or a situation.

Try not to analyse it. State it simply. It could be something like this:

 "Down deep inside…. I'm afraid that….."
(fill in the blanks)

And what does that mean about you?
It means that …………… (your mistaken core belief)

48

Write down the thought or belief that worries, stresses, frustrates or angers you. *(It should be 1-3 sentences long, not more.)*

Now ask yourself:

1. Is it 100% true? How do you feel when you believe it is ?

Ask yourself:

- Am I *dramatizing* the situation and overblowing its importance?
- Am I *generalizing* and assuming things that are not 100% true?
- Am I *over-personalizing* and taking offence at things that are not really related to me?

Now ask yourself again, is my thought or belief 100% true?

✎ YES or ✐ NO

If you consider it true, to what degree is it true? 100%, 75%, 50%, 25%. Giving a general statement that something is true, may be misleading, if it is only 50% true or occasionally, but not always true.

We often give 'truths' a larger power (%) than they are due. If we can demystify it, even for a moment, we loosen the ground upon which it stands. Sometimes, it takes one small doubt, to make the wall start tumbling down.

If your answer is 'Yes', try to 'process' it, to gauge it's actual importance relative to your overall goals.

Imagine: Who could you be if you didn't have that thought? What sort of thoughts would you have instead?

2. Is it kind?

Is your thought of belief kind towards *you*? Are you putting yourself down, being too critical? Self reflection is good, but many times we judge ourselves too harshly. We're all human and we make mistakes; the point is to learn from them, not to let them drain our energy and confidence. (You may find that you can trace back this harsh criticism to your mother or your father's way of disciplining you when you were a child).

Also, is it kind towards the **other**(s)? Look at it from the perspective of the others who are involved. How does the situation look from their perspective? People are not perfect and sometimes they don't realize it. Have you judged them correctly or are you overblowing it? Remember that the goal is to protect *your* mind. The kindness serves *you,* by ridding you of poisonous thoughts.

 Write your thoughts down..

This diagram may assist you in this process by showing how perspective affects our view of truth: What do you see here, an old lady (facing forward), or a young lady (facing to the back). (Image W.E.Hill 1915)

3. Is it useful?

Although fear can sometimes be beneficial, alerting you to real dangers, too much fear and pessimism can poison your mind with self-defeating doubt and paralyze you with indecision. It may also be concealing your deeper desire, or an opportunity. You have to therefore, become a 'witness' to your thought-streams and encourage yourself to think thoughts which are *useful,* in order to keep it healthy and productive.

Consider your thought or belief. What is the benefit of allowing it to run around in your mind? Does it help you in any way? Who would you be if you didn't have it? What would your life look like, if it did not exist? Thoughts that don't pass the test of three should not be taking space in your mind. A ship does not sink from the water around it, but from the water entering it.

And even if the thought is true. Consider; how you can **rephrase, change or modify** it so that it is more Truthful, Kind and Useful, so that it becomes clearer, more positive and more specific?

Write down this new, re-phrased statement in positive terms and read it out loud.

 In psychoanalysis, the Greek myth of the Medusa represents our fears and how we can overcome them through using a "mirror" of self-reflection, in order to get the prizes of *freedom and power*.

Askesis III - DEFINE YOUR ITHACA®
Formulate Your Personal Mission Statement

Background: We face tough decisions everyday. As a parent, spouse, business professional, you encounter several circumstances each day which test your patience, your character and your peace of mind.

A Personal Mission Statement is a *tool that can guide you and help shape your decisions, priorities and reactions, based on your values and the vision you have for your life*. It is a condensed, focused representation of your Ethos. *A helpful reminder from the person you want to be.*

"Give me a place to stand, and I shall move the world"
- Archimedes

Clarifying your life purpose makes it easier to navigate through life, when you have a sense of where you want to go. Your psychological well being is empowered, when your actions and words are aligned with your core values. Life is generally good and you feel more content, confident and satisfied. When your behavior doesn't match your values, you develop a sense of uneasiness that swells inside of you preventing you from reaching your state of eudaimonia.

Externally, leaders are aligned and connected to the mission values and goals of their organization. But internally, leaders must be aligned with a set of personal values and character traits that drive their ultimate success..

In this Askesis you can formulate your Personal Mission Statement, based on your values.

Name: DEFINE YOUR ITHACA®

Purpose: To get clear what are our core values and what this translates into as a personal mission statement, which can guide us through difficulties as an inner compass or GPS.

Instructions: Stage 1. Clarify your Ethos

Answer these 10 questions below to determine your Ethos:

1. Look around your personal and professional spaces. Make a list of 3-5 things that are dear and important to you. Next to each item, write which of the values (from the list below, these things represent. For example: Your University Degree & Certificates of Attendance to Seminars represents 'life-long learning' or 'achievement'. Your Montblanc pen represents 'effectiveness' at getting big contracts or 'elegance'.

2. How do you spend most of your time? Make a list of 3-5 things and next to each item, write which value (from the list below) each thing represents. For example: Working long hours on your computer may represent 'wealth creation'. Going to gym represents health, wellness. Travel may mean adventure for you.

3. What activities energize you? You do these 3-5 activities and you feel *great* afterwards? For example: Jumping on trampoline represents joy, euphoria. Speaking in front of an audience may represent success or strength. Spending regular time with friends could mean loyalty.

4. Where are you spending or investing most of your money?

5. In which area of your life are you most organized, professional, competent, focused and reliable?

6. What are you most obsessed about?

7. What sorts of goals do you set and then able to realize (or notice significant progress over time)?

8. What topics of conversation do you bring up often, or have you taught on. What kind of topics 'energize' you?

9. Who are the celebrities, politicians or people in your life who inspire you?

10. What do you like to learn, listen, study or read about?

 Next to each of the 10 above questions, take note of which of the six core human values these things/activities represent.

The 6 Core Human Values (CHV)

1. **Certainty**: Assurance you can avoid pain and gain pleasure, safety, security.

2. **Uncertainty/Variety**: The need for unknown, change, new stimuli, adventure

3. **Significance**: Feeling unique, of value, important, special or needed, independence.

4. **Connection/Love**: A strong feeling of closeness or union with someone or something.

5. **Growth**: An expansion of capacity, capability or understanding.

6. **Contribution**: A sense of service and focus on helping, giving and supporting others.

Now **arrange these Core Human Values** in order of importance to you, from most important (#1) to least important (#6)

For example, your final list should look something like this:

1. "I love improving lives of others" >> CHV: Contribution

2. "I love travelling." >> CHV: Variety/Uncertainty

3. "I love working in a team." >> CHV: Connection/Love

4. "I love being the boss." >> CHV: Significance

5. "I love to save my money." >> CHV: Certainty

6. "I love taking online courses." >> CHV: Growth

The above are a 'distillation' of your most important values. It reveals to you what experiences really drive and inspire you, 'underneath it all'.

Now, with the above set of your deepest values, you have a clearer picture of "Who you really are...." (Ethos). In order to find fulfillment and to thrive ie eudaimonia, you need to live according to these, in that order of priority. This means to live with **integrity**.

Once you have done the above inner work, only then are you ready to become clear on your personal mission, ie what you are here to do, what has meaning and for whom. Contributing and serving society, your family, your team, your clients, your company, is something that will provide you with a sense of purpose, self respect and self worth. The stuff of which self-leadership will be the natural result, not something you have to strive for.

In his book *"The Leader Who Had No Title"* top management guru, Robin Sharma demonstrates how *we can all work with and influence people like a superstar, regardless of our position. You don't need to be a CEO or a world leader to be a leader from within; You just need to figure out what it is you are skilled at and love to do, and where you can make a difference!*

Instructions: Stage 2 Finding your Mission Statement

Before we proceed to writing your personal Mission Statement, it's useful to gain some clarity on your life's professional mission and purpose by answering these questions:

1. What do I (love to) do? What are my skills and talents? If you could teach someone something, what would that be?

2. Who do I do it *for*?

3. What do those people or causes actually **want** *and* **need** *that I can provide*? What is the **deficiency** or **lack** that you are trying to fulfill? How will it change or transform as a result?

Some guidelines for the formulation of your statement:

- It should be short, preferably contained in one sentence, so that it can be focused, concise and easy to follow.

- It should not be a general, vague or predictable statement. Try to be as *specific* as possible.

- It should be in the present or present-continuous tense. (As if it has already happened.)

- If you are a religious person, you may include your faith within it, if that's what expresses you best.

Here are some examples of mission statements adopted by very successful CEOs.

"To serve as a leader, live a balanced life, and apply ethical principles to make a significant difference." - Denise Morrison, CEO, Campbell Soup Co.

"To have fun in my journey through life and learn from my mistakes." - Sir Richard Branson, Founder, Virgin Group

"To be a teacher. And to be known for inspiring my students to be more than they thought they could be." - Oprah Winfrey, OWN

 Write your own Personal Mission Statement..

When you repeat your Personal Mission Statement, you should, ideally, feel confident about it. It's your personal 'credo', 'motto' or 'maxim'.

Remember that this is a concise distillation of what it takes to make you happy, to allow you to reach your state of Eudaimonia.

You should undertake to repeat your mission statement to keep it current and relevant in your mind. A great way to do that is through guided meditation as explained in the next Askesis "*Morpheas Mind Mechanics*". You should also re-formulate it at regular intervals throughout your life, to update it and adjust for changing circumstances, realities and priorities.

Once you are done, write it on your 'Shield' (below), which you can also 'decorate' with other symbols such as a lion, a sun, a laurel, a crown, anything that will inspire you.

 Suggested to also think about:
What will your obituary in the newspaper look like?

Take a moment to write your obituary or *epitaph;* what you would want written about you when you have passed away many, many years from now. Use words, phrases and sentences. Don't over-think this exercise. Do not edit, censor, analyze or critique your thoughts.

Take 10-15 minutes to complete it. You can revisit it again in the future, so do not try to perfect your answer now. Questions you should ask yourself as you do this exercise are:

- What and/or who did you impact or change? Why?
- What character traits and values did you consistently demonstrate over your life? At your core, who were you?
- Who did you care for? How did you impact or change this person/these people?
- What were major accomplishments in your life? At the ages of 40, 50, 60, 70?
- What did you show interest in? What were you passionate or enthusiastic about?
- What was your legacy?

Think BIG. Imagine possibilities. Ask yourself: *Why not?*

Askesis IV - MORPHEAS MIND MECHANICS®
Program Your Subconscious For Success (audio-mp3)

This basic Askesis, taught within The ALKISTIS Method®, is for inducing a calm, relaxed and harmonious state of body, mind and spirit. It is also conducive to 'programming' the subconscious in realizing a specific "instruction" or "mission", for example a Personal Mission Statement (as discussed in the previous askesis: "*Define Your Ithaca*")

Background: The practice of consciously recognizing and controlling our imagination or dreams, has been around for centuries, since ancient Greek times, when **"*Morpheus*"** the ancient Greek God of Dreams was venerated.

Many temples (Epidaurus, Delphi, Ephesus, and others) contained a special area for 'dream incubation' where pilgrims were induced into a sort of *sleep-trance* for dreaming, with the intention of meeting a particular divinity for the purpose of healing or receiving a message/ insight. (*Hypno-agogia: Greek for* 'Sleep - Channelling')

Image (CC) 2.0: Ancient bronze sculpture of '*Morpheus*', **Greek God of Dreams**. the one with the amazing ability of appearing in dreams of mortals in any form. As his name implies, the Greek word "morphe" means "form" (*meta-morphosis ie*

59

to trans-form). He was the one who shaped and formed dreams. The name of the opiate drug *morphine* is from the name of Morpheus.

Today, modern doctors recommend the daily practice of a deeply relaxing inner state of body and mind, of at least twenty minutes, to help us manage stress and anxiety in a natural, non-chemical way.

Furthermore, scientific studies have proven that in a relaxed state, the mind is more than two hundred (200x!) times more receptive to suggestions, than in its ordinary, conscious state, allowing new thoughts to slip through the defenses of the 'older guard' of thoughts and habits. In addition, when we introduce a 'Personal Mission Statement' (or positive affirmations) during this practice, it can bring on positive, powerful changes in our life. If you are a practicing Christian, Muslim, Buddhist, Hindu, Jew or any other religion, *the Deep Relaxation can also enhance your spiritual experience and euphoria.*

Here are the **benefits** of this Deep Relaxation through Guided Meditation:

- Calms your nerves. Helps you handle stress better in general.

- Cultivates the process of self-induced deep relaxation, so that you can 'relax yourself' at will.

- Increases your mindfulness, allowing you to become more intuitive.

- Offers space to insert a deeply empowering **mission statement** for personal transformation, during the practice..

- Relieves some psychosomatic stress related symptoms.

It's no wonder many professional athletes and top entrepreneurs use these techniques to get outstanding results. (See more in Section 3, Scientific Foundations, Hypno-learning).

When asked about hypnotherapy in an article of the *Harvard Medical School Journal* (Sept. 2015) Dr. Max Shapiro, psychologist, answered that:

"It is now known that the brain has greater ability to influence the body than previously acknowledged... A hypnotic trance empowers people to activate neural circuits that are otherwise hidden... This circuitry can activate greater comfort for pain relief, greater mental focus for certain activities, and greater self-esteem."

Name: MORPHEAS MIND MECHANICS®

Purpose: To get you into a relaxed state, open to suggestion and reprogramming of your subconscious to more positive beliefs and habits.

Instructions: To perform this Askesis you will need to listen to a Guided Meditation (also called Deep Relaxation). There are many on the internet. To start you off you can **download your FREE Deep Relaxation MP3 from the link below:**

http://www.alkistis.net/free_mp3.html

The music on the mp3 has been inspired by original Ancient Greek music. by composer B. Blazoudakis, of The Megaron National Athens Concert Hall, exclusively for The ALKISTIS Method®.

This Askesis, can be done on a daily or weekly basis.

Find a place where you will not be disturbed for 20 minutes. Switch off your mobile devices and close the door, making it clear that you should not be disturbed during the practice.

Lay on a bed, a yoga mat, a carpet or a reclining chair. Cover yourself with a light blanket or throw a jacket over the top part of your body if you are at the office. (This is because it will make you feel more protected, as your temperature drops slightly, during relaxation.)

Lay back, with your legs slightly apart and your arms rested at the sides, preferably with the palms facing upwards.

Play the MP3 audio and simply listen to the soothing voice that will guide you along a beautiful and relaxing inner 'landscape' (for example, a walk along the beach.)

Note: Somewhere around the middle of the mp3, there is a special section where you will be prompted to repeat (mentally) *a suggestive statement.* This is any kind of pre-chosen positive affirmation or mission statement of a result, that is compelling for you - for example, your **Personal Mission Statement or ideal state of being**.

Doing the Deep Relaxation every day, is like watering a 'seed' which will grow and flourish. It will begin to transform your life in a positive way and rewired your brain for success.

Askesis V - THE MAP OF ULYSSES®
Create Your Future Vision

Background: This Askesis will help you get a clearer idea of the ideal version of your future. It defines your *"Ithaca"*, the end experience that you want to achieve. This exercise will help you in three ways:

- First, to define this future vision with more precision, so as to help you take a decision. Decision means precision. Precision focuses our energy.
- Second, to choose the best path which suits your life's reality.
- Third, the clearer you are, the easier it will be to recognise the "Telos" (your desired result) when you see it.

This Askesis is not meant to bind you to a certain result, but to help you become more specific. No one can know what the future holds, and of course you can alter or tweak your vision along the way. So go ahead and don't be afraid to declare what you want- your Ithaca.

The process to create a clear future vision requires three activities:

1. Brainstorming to come up with 2- 3 possible **scenarios, related to the vision that you want.** For each version of these possible scenarios, explore their possible outcomes. For example, you may wish to achieve health, happiness and increased income doing the thing you love most, professionally. But not all scenarios would suit your reality. You will need to find the best fit. In naming the various versions of your mission, you create a map, which will help you find the most ideal route.

2. Deciding which of the 2-3 scenarios is most ideal, by using the decision-making filters of Ethos, Pathos, Logos. View these

scenarios as 'suitors' which may all look good but only one is really the best match for you. Creating a visual representation (Vision Board, Slide-show or a Motivational Mind-Movie video) to view regularly, so as to connect with this vision on a deeper level.

3. Charting achievable goals within a flow-chart, and working from the end goal, the Telos, **backwards** to make it happen.

This way, we allow the Telos (our vision) to guide us.

Name: **THE MAP OF ULYSSES®**

Purpose: Setting a clear destination (*Telos*).

Instructions: First, explore 2-3 possible scenarios that will enable you to achieve your vision for your future. Be as specific as possible. Describe everything in vivid detail:

Where do you want to be living? What will your occupation be? What are your family requirements? What will you see, taste, smell, feel once you have arrived? By when can it realistically be fulfilled? 1 year, 2 years, 3 years, 5 years ahead?

Give each scenario a **title**, so they become more distinguishable in your mind.

You don't have to write full sentences, just **jot down the main points** of your 2-3 scenarios on a separate sheet of paper or a computer screen.

Example*: It is January 2025, and I am living and working in Paris, France. The kids are going to the International School. Me and (spouse or partner's name) are really well and in harmony together. My company is making X turnover and it has been awarded X prize.... My health is great, as I go jogging every day and play volleyball once a week with the team. etc... We also go skiing in the alps once a year. My actions are really making a positive difference to .... and so on...*

Then use the The Alkistis Method® to filter out the most ideal scenario:

ETHOS

1. Does it reflect my character, my **core values** and the **Personal Mission Statement** I created and am committed to?

2. If not, where exactly does it deviate, and what effect will that deviation have on my integrity, prospects, and overall life experience?

3. Does my choice have integrity? Be positive here, but also realistic. Remember, *"To thine own self be true."*

4. Am I ready to change my life, if that's what it takes to achieve this scenario, and will I be happy if I do?

Now the last question - Who will your vision make you become? What does the vision of Ithaca do to you, the Hero?

Carl Jung said that *"The goal is important only as an idea; the essential thing is the opus which leads to the goal: that is the goal of a lifetime."*

PATHOS

1. What **undesired changes** must I make that go against my grain, desired lifestyle or way of doing things? Does it take me out of my comfort zone?

2. What is my greatest **fear, concern,** discomfort or uneasiness about this scenario?

3. What other **emotions** does it inspire in me?

4. What do I really **love** about this particular scenario?

5. Will this scenario really bring more **meaning** to my life?

6. On a scale of 1-10, how **excited** or **moved** am I about this scenario? It should ideally be something like *"HELL YEAH!!!"*

LOGOS

1. Does this scenario actually raise my quality of life? And if so, how?

2. What does this scenario mean for me *financially*? Do I have a clear understanding of the consequences or do I need more research?

3. What things, situations, *lifestyle habits* will I need to change? (Make a list)

4. *Who will these changes affect* except me? (i.e. family members, friends, main stakeholders)

5. Whose *approval* or consent do I need to proceed and will this be easy to get?

6. How large of a *disruption* will this scenario cause in my present life?

7. Do I have a clear plan or *strategy*? What are my milestones? (Make a general 'flow-chart' showing major milestones.)

8. Does it depend on external circumstances or do I have a reasonable *'control'* over the process? How do I minimize risk?

9. What are the greatest *obstacles* for manifesting this scenario?

Also address the other two axis of the Logos trait, namely *Kairos* (timeliness) and *Telos* (end goal)

After this filtering process is complete, it will be easier to **select ONE** of these scenarios, as being the most ideal and compelling one.

 Write down the title of your scenario as if it was a *movie*.

In order to also engage **the right side of your brain in manifesting this scenario** it's recommended to make a visual representation called a "Vision Board". You can do this by using photographs and sticking them onto a collage, or making a 'slideshow' on your computer. Even better is to use audio-visual software to create a 'Motivational Mind-Movie' video, complete with inspiring, upbeat, empowering music and titles.

Apply your imagination with 'role-play'. For example: Some of my clients have even created a 'mock' interview of their future-self by a "reporter from CNN" who asks them about their life and accomplishments, as if it has *already occurred* (in the future year 20XX).

There is no perfect way to do this - have *fun* with it. The point is that, this process will empower you, as well as allow you to address details and consequences, that you may have missed.

When completed, it's recommended you watch it once a week. While watching the vision board, slideshow or motivational mind-movie, try to really imagine that you are in the scene, by engaging all your senses.

Allow yourself to fantasize! The more vividly you can fantasize the better because it will transform the way you see yourself today. You won't feel as stuck when things get tough, because you have already "been to the mountaintop" through your motivational mind-movie.

The best way to predict your future is to create it. Make sure to include all areas of your life. Here is an example:

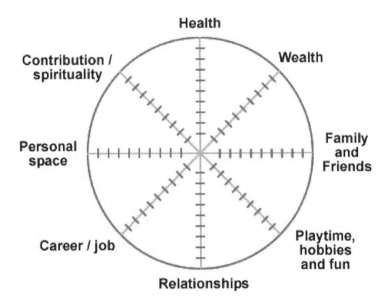

Plotting Your Path To Realize Your Vision On a Flow-Chart.

Another recommended graphical representation to engage the right side of your brain, is plotting out your path towards your vision by creating a big flowchart on a whiteboard or on Excel, or through flow-chart software, or however you want to do it.

Start by defining, on the one end, your present situation, and on the other, the top 5-6 aspects or cornerstones of your end-vision.

The purpose of the flowchart is to help you lay out a road map to get from one place to the other by setting milestones along the way, with specific dates they have to be accomplished by synchronizing the flow and dividing the process into smaller, achievable tasks that will eventually lead to your end vision.

Here is a general idea of what your flow-chart may look like:

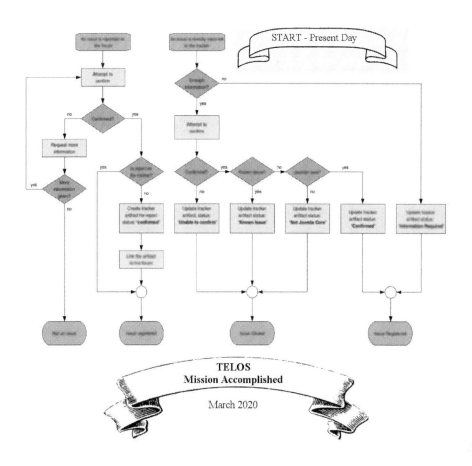

START - Present Day

TELOS
Mission Accomplished

March 2020

꜡꜡꜡꜡꜡꜡꜡

Askesis VI - MASTER OF RHETORIC®
Influence Others With Ease

Background: Persuading others is a very important ability in anything you want to do and can play a great role in achieving your goals and dreams. It is one of the most popular seminars which I am asked to teach, to my corporate clients, because it gives their personnel confidence, effectiveness and facilitates communication and the spread of ideas within the company itself.

The method is the same as we have followed up to now and is explained in Section 1 of this book, Core Concepts, where you read about Aristotle's masterpiece, *The Rhetoric*, where he presents the concepts of Ethos (credibility), Pathos (emotion, imagination) and Logos (logic, reason), as the three traits an orator must have, in order to engage, influence and persuade his audience.

Scientific experiments, including the one conducted by Dr. Albert Mehrabian, Professor Emeritus of Psychology, UCLA, show that Pathos is much more important, when one is trying to influence and persuade others. As can be seen from the chart below, nonverbal communication (body language, eye contact, tone of voice etc) accounts for 93% in importance.

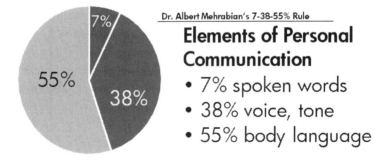

Dr. Albert Mehrabian's 7-38-55% Rule

Elements of Personal Communication
- 7% spoken words
- 38% voice, tone
- 55% body language

The teaching of presentation skills usually requires a coach and a group setting, so that it can be done in a 'real' environment, but you can also explore this yourself, preferably with at least one other person watching you.

In this Askesis you will be standing in front of **a video camera** (and a small group if you are with others) so that you can have a more realistic view of your delivery and impact.

Name: **MASTER OF RHETORIC**®

Purpose: To train and improve our skill of influencing and persuading others.

Instructions: Think about a presentation you want to make in front of a group of people or to someone in particular (your boss, investor, client etc). Think about what you want to persuade or influence them about. What actions do you want them to take?

An example, for addressing a group: *Imagine that shortly, you are going to present yourself to the entrance committee of a very ancient and prestigious school of Self-Leadership. They will be comparing your presentation to hundreds of other applicants. Prepare a presentation, applying Ethos, Pathos, Logos of Aristotle's "Rhetorical Triangle" to convince them to let you join their institution.*

Write down your points to prepare under each principle point:

ETHOS: What is your personal history and integrity in relation to the subject matter? What impressions, qualities or values do you want to leave behind?

 Write down your introduction which should include a greeting, the subject you want to talk about as well as your full name, occupation and relationship to this subject.

Write down the values and impressions you seek to stress.

PATHOS:

 *Write down your **Emotional arguments**:*
"I am really passionate about....." or "I know that you are passionate about...(dreams)...." or "I know that you are concerned about.... (fear)..." Explain your 'Why' in simple words.

LOGOS:

 *Write down your **Logical Arguments**:*
(Show a real life example if possible.)

Conclusion:

 Write down the Summary or Conclusion of your arguments, as a "Call to Action":
Example: *And that's why ....(call to action)...."*

When you have your presentation ready, deliver it to your audience (or to yourself if you can't get anyone) and **film yourself doing it**.

Reviewing the video will tell you a great deal. Focus especially on your body language and other non-verbal communication such as eye-contact, breathing, posture, etc.

- How do you see yourself?
- Do you come across as having the Ethos, Pathos and Logos required to persuade your audience?
- What do the others think?

Repeating this process until you can accept *yourself* as a capable and effective speaker, will greatly improve your chances of *others* seeing you in a similar manner.

Now, About Your Comfort Zone...

Formulating your Ideal, Compelling Future Vision is great, but how is it supposed to happen if we just meditate on it? The answer is - it won't. Realizing your 'Ideal, Compelling Future' needs you to take MASSIVE ACTION... Here is a true story that can inspire you.

In ancient Greece, a young man by the name of Demosthenes, dreamed of becoming a great speaker, but whenever he opened his mouth, he was nervous, awkward, and troubled by both a speech impediment and a stutter. According to Plutarch his speech suffered from *"a perplexed and indistinct utterance and a shortness of breath, which, by breaking and disjointing his sentences much obscured the sense and meaning of what he spoke."*

Demosthenes however was *determined* to be a great speaker, so to overcome his difficulties, he put pebbles in his mouth, to slow himself down, and spoke loudly towards the sea for several hours every day. In time, he eliminated his stutter and overcame his speech impediment. His voice grew louder, stronger, and more confident.

Demosthenes went on to become one of the *greatest and most famous orators in history*. According to one account, when asked to name the three most important elements in oratory, he replied *"Delivery, delivery and delivery!"*

73

What can we learn from this true story?

In order to achieve excellence or even improvement in any area of your life-skills, *you must be willing to move out of your comfort zone*. No movement equals no progress.

As you go through the curriculum and exercises of The ALKISTIS Method®, you must be willing to feel clumsy, awkward and practice regularly, in order for you to move to a higher level of competence.

SECTION 3
Philosophical Foundations

WWW.ALKISTIS.NET

Philosophical Foundations

Image (CC) 2.0 : Raphael's 'School of Athens', in The Vatican, Italy

The ALKISTIS Method® has been particularly inspired by the work of Socrates, Plato, Aristotle as well as the Stoic School.

Although over two millennia have passed since 'The Golden Age' of Greece, (480 BC-320 BC) the legacy of the Greek philosophers can still inspire, motivate and empower us towards success and happiness, a unique state of being, which the Greeks call *Eudaimonia.*

"Eudaimonia" is Human Flourishing

A wonderful Greek word, it literally means,

> *"To be filled with positive spirits."*

76

Eudaimonia is the most sought-after experience for any human who takes their life seriously. It encapsulates 'The Good Life' *here* on Earth, *during* our lifetime; Happiness, Fulfillment, Freedom, Love and Success... *Eudaimonia,* was the raison d'etre of Classical Greek philosophy, and subsequently, it became the foundation of free civilization.

In the **Declaration of Independence of the United States**, Thomas Jefferson writes:

> *"We hold these truths to be self-evident, that all men are created equal, that they are endowed by their Creator with certain inalienable Rights, that among these are Life, Liberty and the pursuit of Happiness."*

The Declaration of Independence, National Archives, Washington D.C.

The US founding fathers stated in the Federalist Papers that:

> *"A good government implies two things: first, fidelity to the object of government, which is the happiness of the people; secondly, knowledge of the means by which that object can be best attained."*

For the Classical Greek philosophers like Socrates, Plato and Aristotle, *happiness is the final end or goal* that encompasses the totality of one's life. It is not something that can be gained or lost in a few hours. It's about playing with a long term strategy.

As Aristotle noted, it is easy enough to see that we desire money, pleasure, and honor only because we believe that these goods will make us happy. It seems that all other goods are a means towards obtaining happiness, while **happiness is always an end in itself.**

Image (CC) 2.0 : The Supreme Court building on Capitol Hill in Washington, D.C., an example of Greek Revival Architecture, completed in 1935. It was designed by Cass Gilbert and built of white marble, exactly like the Parthenon.

The preoccupation of Greek philosophers with developing human potential began around 600 B.C., when there was *a transition from myth to reason.*

The 'magical' world of nymphs and Olympian gods, began giving way to scientific *realism.* It's the reason why so many philosophical and scientific insights originated at that time and place.

Greek philosophers thought deeply, set up public debates and wrote books about *how human beings can take charge of their destiny, reach their full potential and be happy, not in the afterlife, but here on Earth.*

"Happiness depends on ourselves." - **Aristotle**

The concept of *happiness as a basic human right*, may seem obvious to you now, but when the ancient Greeks conceived it, it was a *radical paradigm shift*. No longer were the gods responsible for our happiness, we humans had to take responsibility for our own life.

At that time, when other ancient civilizations, focused on happiness in life *after* death, mainly for royalty, and where vast resources were allocated to creating gigantic pyramids and mausoleums, the Greek philosophers strove to improve the capacity of ordinary citizens, to find happiness in *this* life, not *after* death.

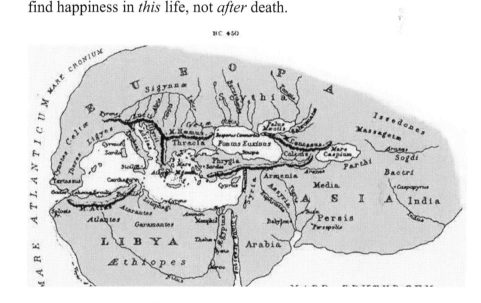

Image (CC) 2.0 : The world according to Herodotus 450 BC

During this 'Golden Era', the Greeks produced some of their highest achievements in the arts and philosophy. The insights they reached are so radical, powerful and important, because they are essential, basic truths that have withstood the test of time, beyond culture, religion and dogma, unifying humankind. It led to them producing such things as Comedy, Democracy, Public Education, the Olympic Games, Freedom of Religion and Trial by Jury...

Areté: The Path of Excellence In Body, Mind & Spirit

In their search for the truth and the ideal way of living, the classical Greek philosophers held the highest esteem for a quality they called **"Areté"**. (Gr. αρετή)

No English word or phrase adequately captures the exact meaning of Areté. The nearest equivalents are **'Excellence'** and **'Virtue'**.

This is what the Greeks believed they should strive for in all their endeavours. *Areté was the pinnacle of their value-system. Especially excellence of character.*

For **Plato**, *Areté* is mainly associated with moral excellence. It involves four specific moral virtues - Prudence, Courage, Temperance and Justice. It's something they all share, a special, *unnamed quality* - their essence. It is clearly related to Goodness, but it's not the same thing.

For **Aristotle**, something is excellent when it *manifests its unique purpose* (Greek: *Telos*). The unique, defining quality of human beings, for Aristotle, what makes them distinct from other animals, is the capacity for rational thought. Human excellence therefore, involves the correct use of reason and logic, principally in connection with a moral choice.

Areté is defined by the perfect balance between two extremes. It is about the right *measure*; the right *proportion*. In ancient Greece, the temple of Apollo at Delphi bore the inscription *Meden Agan* (μηδὲν ἄγαν) - *'Nothing in excess'*. It is the wise path; the middle way. It doesn't mean mediocrity. It means that when it comes to fear for example, *courage* is the virtuous path, the one with *areté*, and not *cowardice* or *recklessness*.

The teachings of that age still guide us today and have become the motto of many academic, political and other institutions all over the world.

"ΑΙΕΝ ΑΡΙΣΤΕΥΕΙΝ" ... "Ever To Excel"

Image (CC) 2.0: Boston College Library has the motto: "ΑΙΕΝ ΑΡΙΣΤΕΥΕΙΝ"

The above phrase is derived from Homer's famous epic the Iliad; It is used in a speech Glaucus delivers to Diomedes. During a battle between the Greeks and Trojans, Diomedes is impressed by the bravery of the mysterious young man and demands to know his identity. Glaucus replies:

> *"Hippolochus begat me. I claim to be his son, and he sent me to Troy with strict instructions: Ever to excel, to do better than others, and to bring glory to your forebears, who indeed were very great ... This is my ancestry; this is the blood I am proud to inherit."*

Take a moment to feel the power of that phrase.

They are the words of a young man, a brave warrior, who *knows who he is and knows what his values are. He has self-leadership, and a clear sense of purpose.* This is something much deeper than having mere 'self-confidence', it is *Areté,* excellence.

To a person of Areté (moral excellence) there are few dilemmas. Their character is their guide.

According to the Greek philosophers, Areté is what we must all strive for, everyday of our lives, for our own benefit, because it's the only way to reach Eudaimonia. As Aristotle says,

"We are what we repeatedly do ...
Excellence is therefore a habit."

 Take a moment to self-reflect on your thoughts about the path to *Eudaimonia* through *Areté*.

Following is a short summary of **Socrates**, **Plato** and **Aristotle**, the three great classical philosophers known as the 'Classic Trio', as well as the school of **Stoicism** which followed them. This is by no means an overview of all their teachings, but only the insights that inspired The ALKISTIS Method®.

Socrates

"Know thyself."
*(Ancient inscription at the temple of Apollo in Delphi,
Greece adopted by Socrates as his motto.)*

Socrates was born in Athens, Greece in 460 BC and has a unique place in the history of happiness and personal well-being as he is *the first known figure in history to argue that happiness is actually obtainable through human effort.*

Like most ancient peoples, the Greeks had a rather pessimistic view of human existence. Happiness was deemed a rare occurrence and *reserved only for those whom the gods favored.* The idea that one could pursue happiness for oneself was considered *hubris*, a kind of overreaching pride and was to be met with harsh punishment by the gods. Many Greek myths warned of this horrible fate.

Against this fatalistic backdrop, the optimistic Socrates enters the scene. The key to happiness, he argues, is to turn attention away from the body and towards the mind's inner world. *By self-inquiry and the harmonizing of our desires, we can learn to pacify the mind*

83

and achieve a state of inner tranquility. According to Socrates, leading a moral life is to be preferred to an immoral one, *primarily* because it leads to happiness.

We see right here, at the beginning of Western philosophy, that happiness is at the forefront, linked to other concepts such as virtue, justice, discernment. It is central in understanding the ultimate meaning of human existence, beyond religion.

The Roman Stoic philosopher Cicero once said that Socrates: *"..Wrestled philosophy from the heavens and brought it down to Earth."* One could say he was a sort of *Prometheus* - taking fire from the gods and giving it to humans, thus giving them the tool to determine their own destiny. Prior to Socrates, Greek philosophy consisted primarily of metaphysical or scientific questions, such as: *Why does the world stay up, suspended in space? Is the world composed of one substance or many substances?*

But living amidst the horrors of the Peloponnesian War, when Athens had lost to Sparta, Socrates was more interested in essential *existential, ethical* and *social* issues: *What is the best way to live? Why be moral when immoral people seem to benefit more? Do the rich live better than the poor? Is happiness about satisfying one's deep desires or is it about being good and acting with honor?*

According to Socrates, examining oneself, our motives and actions, is the most important task one can undertake. Self-observation alone, will give us the knowledge necessary to answer the question **'How should I live my life?'**

When we turn our gaze inwards and focus on self-knowledge, Socrates proposed, we will soon discover our true nature and potential. And contrary to the opinion of the masses, one's True Self according to Socrates is not to be identified with what we own, with our social status, professional achievements or even with one's own body. Socrates believed that philosophy had a very important role to play in the lives of individuals on a very fundamental level:

*"For you see what our discussions are all about and is
there anything about which a man of even small
intelligence would be more serious about than this:
What is the way we ought to live?* - **Socrates**

The Pursuit of Happiness According to Socrates

*"Most excellent men, are you not ashamed to care for
the acquisition of wealth and for reputation and honor,
when you neither care nor take thought for wisdom and
truth in the perfection of your soul... "*
- **Socrates** (The Apology, Plato 399 BC)

All human beings naturally strive after happiness, thought Socrates, for the pursuit of happiness *(Eudaimonia)* is the greatest goal in our life. And everything we do, we do because we think it will make us happy. We therefore *label* what we think will bring us happiness as 'good'. And those things we think will bring us suffering and pain we label as *'bad'*.

So it follows, that if we have a mistaken conception of what is good, then we will spend our lives frantically chasing after things that will not bring us happiness, *even if we attain them.* Socrates has been proven right after all, by modern science: *Scientific surveys in many countries over decades proved that most blue-collar working people are just as happy as rich people, and teenagers from working class families describe themselves as happier than teenagers from affluent families.*

The point here is that obtaining wealth and power are fine but are not ends in themselves. We must also satisfy our soul, which seeks love, connection, contribution, harmony in order to be truly fulfilled. That may seem obvious, but how many of us have lost track of what is really valuable and good for us, in our pursuit for the stars? And on the same note, concerning the quality of life our achievements offer us, how many of us have the time or peace to actually enjoy it?

According to Socrates, if one devoted themselves to mindfulness (in Greek = *prosoche*) and sincere inquiry, they will soon be led to a more appropriate view of what is Good and how to attain happiness and success.

There is one Supreme Good, he claimed, and possession of this alone will secure our happiness. This Supreme Good is obtained through *Moral Excellence, Virtue, Honor, "Areté"*.

Areté: The path to Eudaimonia

If one is pursuing well-rounded happiness, one cannot avoid *Areté*. It is the 'fast-track' to fulfillment and personal success.

An individual is considered virtuous, if their character is made up of the moral qualities that are accepted as the highest human qualities. They are the Four Cardinal Virtues: *courage, temperance, prudence, and justice.* They were living values, taught in schools and in the Olympic Games of Ancient Greece.

This concept can be summarized as follows:

Areté (Moral Excellence + Virtue + Honor)
=>> **Eudaimonia** (Happiness + Success)

But if all individuals naturally desire happiness, and if it is only by becoming virtuous that one can attain happiness, then a simple question arises - *Why do so many people fail to become virtuous and instead choose to commit 'bad' acts?*

Socrates maintained that the answer to this question is *that these people are ignorant.* If they truly knew that what they are doing was 'evil' and the repercussions it has on their happiness, they would refrain from such actions. It would actually be in their self interest to do so, because they would understand that only if they were virtuous could they be truly happy.

Socrates held that all evil acts are committed in ignorance… About 500 years later, Jesus Christ was to say *"Forgive them Father, for they know not what they have done."* Of course, that does not mean we will not fight to avoid or stop people from harming us, but at least we do not have to respond in the same way. We must do what is in *our* benefit, retain our virtue and composure and not let toxic people drain our energy from us.

The Originator of Authentic, Servant Leadership

Socrates can be acknowledged as the originator of "Authentic, Servant Leadership" which is a tendency more and more nowadays in enterprises and organizations since the 60's. This is an approach to leadership that emphasizes building the leader's legitimacy through honest relationships, built on an ethical foundation, with followers whose input is valued.

> *"The way to gain a good reputation is to endeavor to be what you desire to appear." - Socrates*

The person you want to be true to is *yourself*, not what others want of you, or the false image you have had to adopt to please or intimidate others. As Shakespeare wrote in Hamlet, *"To thine own self be true."* You must strive to present this true image to the world. This is what 'Ethos' dictates and this is what is also best for *you*.

A lot of unhappiness and stress is caused by pretending you are someone that you are not. Socrates warns against that. Although you may have to do this on occasion to advance your interests, you must try to avoid falsehood as much as possible, because it can have dire consequences; not only for others or for the society that you and your loved ones live in, but for you, personally, and your well-being.

No one can dispute that our professions may give us our daily subsistence, but we need to strike a balance between our personal 'standards' and what is required for results. Authenticity is an art and a goal well worth pursuing.

Achieving this authenticity is an ongoing process that involves mindfulness *prosoche* and the exercising of vigilant questioning of the world and our beliefs, to test if they hold true. By applying this simple but radical approach to understanding, Socrates turned the history of human thought on its head. His approach was what we now famously call *The Socratic Approach*.

The Socratic Approach

"Socrates... was one of the greatest philosophers the world has ever known. He did something that only a handful of people in all history have been able to do; he sharply changed the whole course of human thought; and now twenty-four centuries after his death, he is honored as one of the wisest persuaders who ever influenced this wrangling world..."
- **Dale Carnegie**, Pioneer in modern leadership training

Socrates created *the first recorded rational approach to personal development* at a time when mysticism and dogma were the standard. He believed that we can only arrive at the truth by questioning our own assumptions, on a regular basis.

**"I cannot teach anyone anything,
I can only teach them to think." - Socrates**

According to Socrates, what often causes suffering is our own misguided and *irrational* beliefs. We are our own imprisoners, our own torturers, we cling to our toxic, self-sabotaging beliefs, even when they hurt us. The consequences of an unexamined life are tremendous.

"An unexamined life is not worth living." - Socrates

So how do we free ourselves from the self-made prisons we've constructed in our minds?

Socrates taught that what we need to do is *learn how to ask ourselves critical questions;* not just assume that our 'mind chatter', the generalizations and preconceptions we hold, are always true. Socrates taught that we shouldn't believe everything we think. On the contrary, he taught that it's often self-deception in the form of a 'lie' or a 'distortion of the truth'. We need to constantly question and test our thinking, to arrive at the truth or the solution.

Harvard professor of 'Emotional Intelligence' Daniel Goleman, analyses this phenomenon in his book *'Vital Lies, Simple Truths - The Psychology of Self - Deception'*. The art is in maintaining our objectivity; being able to observe our own self in order to become aware of how our attitude, intention and behaviour participate in the formation of the problems we are actually trying to solve.

So what exactly was Socrates' approach? Did he tell people they were wrong? Of course not, that's for amateurs. He was a master. His whole technique consisted of a series of questions. Also known as *'The Socratic Method'*, it was based upon setting up a debate or dialogue for getting to the *objective truth.*

He strategically asked questions to which his 'opponent-doubter' would have to agree. As he kept on winning one admission after another, he put the person in a 'positively-inclined' state ie open to accepting the objective truth. He kept on asking questions until finally, almost without realizing it, his 'opponent-doubters' found themselves embracing a conclusion they would have bitterly denied just a few minutes earlier.

In a study, published in the Huffington Post, by Don Joseph Goewey, subjects were asked to write down their worries over an extended period of time and then identify which of their imagined misfortunes did not actually happen:

"Lo and behold, it turns out that 85 percent of what subjects worried about, never happened, and with the 15 percent that did happen, 79 percent of subjects discovered either they could handle the difficulty better than expected, or the difficulty taught them a lesson worth learning. This means that 97 percent of what you

worry over is not much more than a fearful mind punishing you with exaggerations and misperceptions."

That's not to say you shouldn't worry. Fear keeps you vigilant; it forces you to think, and take action. But too much fear is paralyzing and stops you from taking the path you should take. As with everything, there must be balance. *Courage is a virtue. Cowardice and recklessness are vices.*

 Let us take a moment to apply Socrates's simple method as regards to generalizations we hold true. Based on the Socratic Approach we need to ask, *'Is this generalization true?"* Perhaps it was true once, but no longer is or it may not be true at all. Using Logos, do this exercise below:

1. Take a general belief you have about yourself, others, your environment, or the world in general. A perspective, such as: "One has to sweat for his daily bread; nothing comes easy", or "One can never really trust one's employees", or "Politicians are only looking after their interests."

2. Search to find one exception to this general statement. e.g. . "One has to sweat for his daily bread; nothing comes easy, except for that time, when that deal came right into my lap", or "All employees are not trustworthy, but there was one employee in particular who proved that was very trustworthy, beyond any doubt', or "All politicians are looking after their own interests, but so-and-so wasn't."

3. If such a (new, truer) statement is formulated, then this means that the (original) 'general' statement was *imprecise* and is discredited. This opens the way for more exceptions of the (original) general statement. One exception can dislodge our (false) belief and free us of its 'chains'.

4. We need to therefore ask that part in us which made the generalization to take this exception(s) into consideration, or at least let it co-exist with it.

When we have dislodged the first stone, we can then keep ourselves open to finding other examples and slowly come to formulate a statement much closer to the truth. This gives us a better and more in depth understanding of reality.

The Socratic Approach of questioning the truth of everything we think, will also lead us to a better understanding of *ourselves* and *our authentic* needs and wants.

Wisdom from Within

In Plato's books *Apology 31c*, and in *Republic 496* and without giving a full explanation, Socrates refers to an 'inner voice' called 'Daimonion' (δαίμων - literally translates into 'an inspiring spirit') which warned him of dangers but never told him what to do:

> *I have a divine sign [daimonion] from the god which... began when I was a child. It is a voice, and whenever it speaks it turns me away from something I am about to do, but it never turns me towards anything. This is what has prevented me from taking part in public affairs, and I think it was quite right to prevent me. Be sure, gentlemen of the jury, I should have died long ago otherwise.*

What he seems to mean by this is that, apart from relying on analytical reasoning to lead your life, you should also listen to your inner voice, your *intuition*, when it warns you of dangers you can't see. This is intricately linked to what Aristotle referred to as *Pathos*.

It's good advice. Intuition is an *instinct* developed through countless generations of humans that survived through trouble and hardship, and should always be taken into account when reaching a decision, after, of course, being analysed as to whether it's true (*Logos*).

Plato

*"For man to conquer himself is the
first and noblest of all victories."* - **Plato**

Born in 428 BC, into a prominent and wealthy family in the city state of Athens, Plato was an aristocratic man with superb athletic physique. His real name is thought to have been Aristocles; Plato may have been a nickname, either given to him by his wrestling coach in reference to his broad shoulders (in Greek 'Platon' means *broad*), or because of his broad intellect or forehead.

He studied under Socrates and then devoted his life to one goal; helping people reach a state of what he termed *'eudaimonia'* meaning success, happiness and fulfillment.

Like his teacher Socrates, Plato thought that the truth could not be reduced to simple formulas, and then just "applied", whenever it's convenient. Rather, it had to be discovered by each person for themselves; but not in isolation. Partners and dialogue are indispensable. It requires a process. It's why all his writings are in the form of dialogues (Greek; *dia* through and *logues* words, logic) -

imaginary discussions, in which Socrates, his mentor, is always given a starring role in conversing and debating issues.

For Plato, however, true insights come from a timeless sphere of eternal truths; the world of Ideas; a higher world, of which this material world that we perceive is just a *shadow*. In order to find happiness, Plato maintained, we need to have the Guiding Light of the Idea of True, Eternal Love and Goodness.

> *"Be kind, for everyone you meet*
> *is fighting a hard battle."* - **Plato**

Among his over 36 works are *The Republic, The Symposium, The Laws, The Meno,* and *The Apology.* Most of them have the purpose of showing how these high ideals and ethics can be applied to our private life and politics, for a just and civilized society. For example in *The Republic*, Plato was the first person in history to contend that people had a right to free education by the *State,* that women too should be educated, and that women would make just as good rulers as men. These were revolutionary proposals at the time and in many places of the world, they still are.

Plato contributed several very powerful insights for making life more fulfilling, which concern us.

The Cave Allegory: Prisoners of our Thoughts

We rarely give ourselves time to think carefully and logically about our lives and how to live them. Apart from our own inner 'beliefs' which we hold true, we often just go along with popular opinions, like 'Fame is great', 'Money is Power' etc. In the 36 books he wrote, Plato showed this common sense to be filled with errors, prejudice and superstition. Plato's answer, like his teacher Socrates, is to *"Know Thyself"* - or at least try. To do so means the beginning of self inquiry.

Expressing his more metaphysical nature, Plato maintained that our body is nothing more than a vehicle for the soul, a sort of *biological virtual reality suit*. Through philosophy, we could expand our mind and come to the realization that what we perceive as reality is only a shadow of a greater reality. He explained this concept in his work, *The Republic,* using a simple allegory; the Allegory of the Cave. *It illustrates the need for more self-reflection and self-knowledge and the consequences of not doing so.*

Description of the Cave Allegory: *In a fictional dialogue between Socrates (Plato's teacher) and Glaucon (Plato's brother), Socrates describes a scenery deep in a cave where a group of people have lived since infancy. These people have always been chained in such a way that they cannot move their heads in any other direction, than to a blank wall in front of them. Behind them there is a fire and between the fire and them, there is a path on which other people pass, holding up various objects. The shadows of these objects, project on the wall, but not the shadows of the people carrying them. The chained people see the moving objects and begin to ascribe forms and meaning to them.*

When one of them is freed and shown the reality outside the cave, he comes to understand that the shadows on the wall do not reflect reality at all. From this point on, he can perceive the true form of reality (e.g. the true objects) rather than the mere shadows seen by the prisoners.

According to Plato, every prisoner that was freed also had the obligation to return to the cave and help free the other prisoners, although he may be mocked by them and even have to face hostility. This stresses the social responsibility aspect of Self-inquiry and Self-reflection.

> **"The measure of a man is what he does with power."**
> **- Plato**

Subjecting your view of reality to examination, rather than accepting it at face value, as we do for so many things, along with the rest of the 'cave dwellers', is the path of the wiser leader (the philosopher - king). The more you understand the true reality of the world around you and inside you, the less the decisions you make will be affected by your biases, preconceptions, superstitions and emotions, something Plato compares to being *dragged around by wild horses*.

We often do *at least one of three things* with incoming sensory information; delete, distort, or generalise. Often we do varying combinations of all three. Here is a guideline on the three mental chains we often foster, that create a lack of perspective:

Deletion – Omitting certain aspects of our experience by selectively paying attention, focusing on specific parts, and deleting the rest from our conscious awareness.

Distortion – Distorting our experience, leading to being frightened of a harmless situation, or being intimidated by certain people, and misinterpreting what is being said.

Generalisation – Drawing conclusions about ourselves, others or situations in general, based on a particular personal experience, hearsay, or other trends of thought.

The Charioteer Allegory: Self Leadership

From Plato also comes the vision of the three-part nature of the soul, or psyche, as explained through the *allegory of the charioteer.* A concept with great depth, it furnishes an unmatched visualization of what a human is, and why he does what he does.

The Charioteer represents reason, the part of the soul that must guide itself to truth and happiness (Eudaimonia). One horse represents rational or moral impulse, the positive part of passionate nature (e.g. *honor, righteous indignation*), while the other represents the soul's irrational passions, appetites, and lustful nature.

Without expanding into Plato's metaphysical descriptions, the purpose of the Charioteer is to direct the entire chariot, ie the soul, towards *enlightenment,* while keeping the horses aligned and in balance, a difficult task, given that one wants to rise to the heavens, and the other to return to earth.

The Greeks saw these elements of the soul as real forces, like electricity that could move a man to act and think in certain ways. Each element has its own motivation and desires: Reason seeks truth and knowledge. Passion seeks food, drink, sex and material wealth. Honor seeks glory and recognition with modesty and temperance.

Plato believed Reason to be the loftiest aim, but each force, if properly harnessed and employed, becomes part of our self-mastery and can contribute to a person's *Eudaimonia.* Achieving this harmony of soul and self-alignment, Plato argues, is a precursor to tackling any other endeavors in life, like leading others.

This powerful concept of the Charioteer is borrowed by The ALKISTIS Method® to help visualize the relationship between Ethos, Pathos and Logos, since they represent a similar dynamic.

Aristotle

"Educating the mind without educating the heart,
is no education at all."
— **Aristotle,** *'Rhetoric'* 4th century BC

Aristotle is one of the greatest thinkers in the history of western science and philosophy, making contributions to logic, metaphysics, mathematics, physics, biology, botany, ethics, politics, agriculture, medicine, dance and theatre. He was a student of Plato, who in turn studied under Socrates.

Aristotle was born around 384 B.C. in the ancient Greek Kingdom of Macedonia, where his father was the royal doctor. He grew up to be arguably the most influential philosopher who ever lived, with many nicknames like *'The Master'*, or simply *'The Philosopher'*.

His first big teaching commission was tutoring Alexander The Great, to whom he taught his leadership skills. When Alexander the Great went out to conquer the whole of the known world, Aristotle headed off to Athens, to study under Plato for a while, until eventually branching out on his own.

In 335 BC, he founded the *Lyceum*, the first scientific institute, based in Athens, Greece. He was one of the strongest advocates of a liberal arts education, which stresses the education of the whole person, including one's moral character, rather than merely learning a set of skills. According to Aristotle, this view of education is necessary if we are to produce a society of happy, as well as productive individuals. For Aristotle, philosophy was about practical wisdom being of service to society.

What Makes People Happy ?

> *"All people seek one goal; Eudaimonia (Success and Fulfillment)... The only way to achieve true success is to express yourself completely in service to society... First, have a definite, clear, practical ideal - a goal, an objective. Second, mobilize the necessary resources to achieve your ends; wisdom, money, materials, and methods. Third, adjust all your means to that end..." -*
> **Aristotle**

More than anybody, Aristotle enshrines happiness as the central purpose of human life and a goal in itself. As a result he devotes more space to the topic of happiness, than any thinker prior to the modern era. He too, like Socrates and Plato before him, concluded that happiness depends on the cultivation of virtue (*Areté*). Aristotle was convinced that a genuinely happy life required the fulfillment of a broad range of conditions, including physical as well as mental well being. In this way, and being of a practical nature, he introduced the idea of a *science of happiness*, in the classical sense, as a new field of knowledge.

Essentially, Aristotle argues that virtue is achieved by maintaining the 'Golden Mean', which signifies moderation; the *balance between two excesses*. Aristotle's doctrine of the Mean is reminiscent of the teachings of many religions, such as Buddha's Middle Path. It was a widely accepted idea. As inscribed on the temple of Apollo at Delphi, *"μηδεν αγαν"*; "nothing in excess" (meaning self-mastery, not mediocrity).

One of Aristotle's most influential works is the *Nicomachean Ethics*, where he presents a theory of happiness, that is still relevant today, over 2,300 years later. The key question Aristotle seeks to answer in these lectures is *"What is the ultimate purpose of human existence?"* In other words, what is that end or goal toward which we should direct all of our activities?

Everywhere we see people seeking pleasure, wealth, fame and honor. But while each of these has some value, none of them can take the place of the ultimate good, that which humanity should aim for. Towards that ultimate end, an act must be self-sufficient and final, to be *"that which is always desirable in itself and never for the sake of something else"* (Nicomachean Ethics, 1097a30-34), and it must also be attainable by man.

Aristotle claims that nearly everyone would agree, that happiness is the end which meets all these requirements. It is easy enough to see that we desire money, pleasure, fame and honor only because we believe that these goods will make us happy. It seems that all other goods are a *means towards obtaining happiness, while happiness is always an end in itself.*

In the *Nicomachean Ethics*, Aristotle suggested that good and truly successful people all possessed distinct virtues. He proposes that we should become better at identifying what these are, so that we can nurture them in ourselves and honor them in others.

He zeroed in on eleven basic virtues as a guideline over 2000 years ago: *courage, temperance, liberality, magnificence, magnanimity, pride, patience, truthfulness, wittiness, friendliness and modesty.* Indeed, not a bad mix of attributes to possess as a leader, whether one is a CEO, a politician, or a parent in today's world.

Balance in Character and The Middle Path

Expanding on the idea of balance, Aristotle also observed that every virtue, seems to be smack in the middle of two vices. It occupies what he termed - the 'Golden Mean' between two extremes of character. In book four of his ethics under the charming title of, *'Conversational Virtues, Wit, Buffoonery, Boorishness'* Aristotle looks at ways people are better or worse at conversation. Knowing how to have a good conversation is one of the key ingredients of the good life, Aristotle recognized. Who can argue with that?

Some people go wrong because they lack a subtle sense of humor and that's *'the boor'*; someone useless for any kind of social intercourse because he contributes nothing and takes offense at everything. But others carry humor to excess; *'the buffoon'* cannot resist the joke sparing neither himself nor anybody else. This character will try to provoke laughter saying things that a man of taste would never dream of saying...

So the virtuous person is in the 'golden mean' in this area; witty but tactful. Definitely an art to be shared, Aristotle even drew up a table of too little, too much and just right around a whole host of virtues. He wrote,

> *"Anybody can become angry - that is easy, but to be angry with the right person and to the right degree and at the right time and for the right purpose, and in the right way - that is not within everybody's power and is not easy."*

Moral goodness, and happiness says Aristotle, is a *result of habit*. It takes time, practice, and encouragement, so Aristotle thinks people who lack virtue should be understood as being unfortunate rather than being wicked. (As if they have a 'disability'.)

What they need isn't scolding or being thrown into prison but better teachers and more guidance. We need to protect ourselves from disabled people, not attack them, and we need to expand our understanding of others. Self-leadership is an art which includes the understanding of oneself and others. (See chart on next page.)

We can't change our behavior in any of these areas at the drop of a hat, but change is possible eventually, especially if we have a deep desire to improve ourselves.

"We are what we repeatedly do.
Excellence is therefore a habit." - **Aristotle**

The table in the next diagram depicts the path of virtue, Aristotle's *Golden Mean* expressing the balance between deficiency and excess.

DEFICIENCY of VIRTUE (vice)	VIRTUE	EXCESS of VIRTUE (vice)
Cowardice	Courage	Rash
Insensible	Temperance	Dissipation
Stinginess	Generosity	Wastefulness
Chintzy	Magnificence	Vulgar
Aspersion	Magnanimity	Vainglory
Indolence	Industrious	Overambitious
Indifference	Caring	Controlling
Self-deprecation	Honest	Boastfulness
Boorishness	Charming	Buffoonery
Quarrelsome	Friendliness	Obsequious
Lying	Truthful	Tactless
Impatient	Tolerant	Doormat
Timid	Confident	Domineering
Fickle	Loyal	Gullible
Unsure	Vigilant	Impetuous
Cowardice	Protective	Bully
Fearful	Patient	Impulsive
Rudderless	Flexible	Rigid
Naïve	Practical	Cynical
Wimpy	Assertive	Arrogant
Selfish	Nurturing	Martyr
Paranoid	Confident	Arrogant
Pushover	Careful	Stubborn

The Art of Persuasion for Leaders

Like many people, Aristotle was struck by the fact that the best argument doesn't always win a debate. He wanted to know - why does this happen and what can we do about it? He had lots of opportunities for observation.

In Ancient Athens, many decisions were made in public meetings often in the Agora (the open marketplace) of the town square. Orators would vie with one another to sway popular opinion. Aristotle observed the ways audiences and individuals are influenced by many factors that don't strictly engage with logic or the facts of the case. It's irritating, and the reason many serious people tended to avoid the marketplace and populous debate.

So, Aristotle wrote the *first ever manual on the art of persuasion*. He called it *'The Rhetoric'*. We already discussed in the introduction. In it he presents the concepts of *Ethos, Pathos,* and *Logos,* as the traits an orator must have in order to influence and persuade his audience.

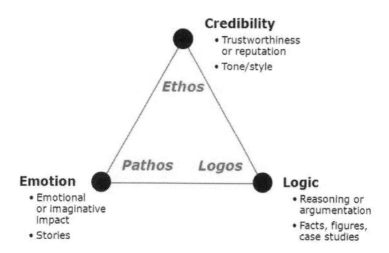

He also referenced two more, lesser known traits, that of *Telos* (ending), meaning the purpose or attitude of a speech, and *Kairos* (time, weather), meaning the particular setting, context, atmosphere, time, and place that a speech occurs.

It is these concepts and their extended application to ourselves that form the backbone of The ALKISTIS Method®.

Stoicism

"Just keep in mind — the more we value things outside our control, the less control we have" - Epictetus

On a warm afternoon, around 300 BC, a haggard, long faced man paced the streets of ancient Athens. He had never been a joyful figure, but he was especially sullen today as he had suffered a great loss. His name was Zeno and he had been a wealthy merchant, until recently. Then on a voyage from Phoenicia to Piraeus (the port of Athens) his ship sunk in the rough, stormy waters of the Aegean sea. He managed to survive, but lost everything he had.

Stopping by a book-shop, he browsed "Memorabilia", a scroll by Xenofon, detailing the teachings of the father of Greek philosophy, Socrates. So impressed was he at these insights, he asked the book-seller where men like this might be found.

Just then, Crates of Thebes, the most famous Cynic living at that time in Greece happened to be walking by. The bookseller pointed. "Follow him..." he advised Zeno.

As so Stoicism began - with a businessman and a cynic. They were men hardened by life, searching for truth and wisdom, and **a way to be happy, no matter what difficulties life may throw at them**.

As with all other schools of thought, Stoicism was greatly influenced by the teachings of those before them, like Socrates, Plato, Aristotle and others. Famous philosophers of Stoicism include Zeno of Citium, a former slave, Epictetus, the Roman Emperor Marcus Aurelius, the Roman statesman Seneca The Younger, and the arch-enemy of Julius Caesar, Cato the Younger. The wide variety of these, demonstrates that Stoicism is applicable to all walks of life.

The term "stoic" was taken from the "stoa poikile", meaning "painted colonnade" (in the 'Agora' ie marketplace) where Zeno used to teach, instead of at the more established lyceums and academies. (In modern times, we often use the word 'stoic' referring to someone who remains calm under pressure and avoids emotional extremes.)

The ancient Stoics prided themselves on being rational, objective thinkers. They believed that humanity's greatest asset is a functional mind and to exercise reason is the most virtuous pursuit. Their "physics", i.e. their view of the world, may have some errors compared to what we know today, but that was only because it was an attempt to rationally explain the world *given the facts they had at the time*, without depending on mysticism. They would be the first to adopt today's scientific insights and adjust their views accordingly because they were what we would call 'mature, grown-ups'. Stoics take full responsibility for their life, and they base their views on science, logic and reason.

You might ask, where does love fit into this equation? Stoics believe that if we all thought more rationally we would all be less egotistical. There would be alot more love in this world: Love for each other, love for the environment and love for ourselves. Why? Because it makes sense - we all win in a more loving and just society.

The philosophy asserts that only Virtue is capable of bringing true happiness and fulfillment. Virtue (ie ethical and moral well-being), is living in agreement with Nature, and practicing the Four Cardinal Virtues (from Socrates/Plato's teachings):

- **phronêsis** (Practical Wisdom - knowing good from bad)

- **dikaiosunê** (Justice, fairness, and kindness in our relations with others.)

- **andreia** (Wise courage and endurance in response to our pain and anxiety.)

- **sôphrosunê** (Temperance - Wise self-discipline in response to our desires.)

As an ethical doctrine, the goal of Stoicism is freedom from anguish or suffering, through the pursuit of reason and "apatheia" (Greek word meaning dispassionate, objective, unemotional reaction, and clear judgment). It teaches indifference and a "passive" reaction to external events on the grounds that nothing external can be good or evil, because it depends on how we view things .

Stoicism therefore gives us back the power, offering equanimity in the face of life's highs and lows.

Socrates was their hero and 'role-model'. He was put on trial accused of corrupting the youth of Athens. After being found guilty of this charge, he was sentenced to death. As he is being held in prison, his old friend Crito comes to see him and provides Socrates with an opportunity to escape. Socrates refuses to escape and accepts his impending death, making a choice in keeping with his values and character.

The Three Disciplines

There are *three* areas of application of Stoic philosophy:

The Discipline of Assent. (Greek: *Sunkatathesis*) This has to do with how we allow ourselves to perceive the world around us. When we control our perceptions, we get mental clarity; the ability to

106

assent to true impressions, dissent from false ones, and suspend our judgment (*epoché* ie Greek for 'suspension of judgment') toward uncertain ones. It concerns how we should judge our impressions so as not to be carried away by them into anxiety or disturbing emotions. (*See Askesis I and II*)

The Discipline of Desire (Greek: *Orexis*) Teaches us about what is best to want or avoid. What should our goals be? Where do we channel our energy, time and resources. This has to do with how we align and apply our desire with the course of Nature; A wise person would seek to harmonize his inner *Logos,* with the greater cosmic *Logos,* just like a musician attunes his/her instrument to the symphony orchestra. When we do this, we can deal with anything the world puts before us.

The Discipline of Action. (Greek: *Hormê*) This has to do with the actions we take or do not take towards a desired outcome; when we direct our actions properly and justly, we are effective and get results. The discipline has to do with the development of the skill to take the right action *(Kathekon)*, at the right time *(Kairós)*, for the right reason *(Orthos logos)*. It also helps us in the social sphere; How do we behave towards others?

Vincit qui se vincit.
(Stoic motto, Latin: He conquers, who conquers himself)

Let's look at how these three main disciplines would look in practice:

The Discipline of Assent

1. Immediately **recognize what is in or out of your control.**

   A stoic realizes that only his/her thoughts and intentions are truly within their sphere of control; everything else is ultimately uncontrollable.

   "The chief task in life is simply this: to identify and separate matters so that I can say clearly to myself which

107

are externals and not under my control, and which have to do with the choices I actually control. Where then do I look for good and evil? Not to uncontrollable externals, but within myself to the choices that are my own."
            - Epictetus, Discourses, 2.5, 4-5

The 'Dichotomy of Control', is a central idea that the Stoics held and practiced. It is also the original concept behind the Christian Serenity Prayer,

"God, grant me the serenity to accept the things that I can not change, the courage to change the things I can, and the wisdom to know the difference".

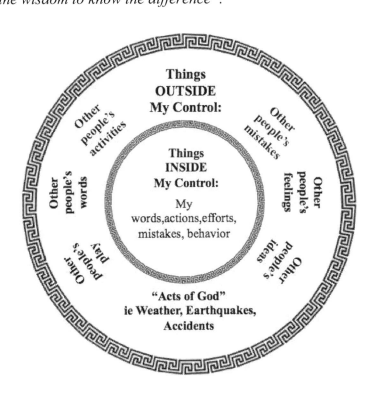

Here is how Epictetus puts it in his Enchiridion (a sort of Stoic manual):

"Some things are within our power, while others are not. Within our power are opinion, motivation, desire,

aversion and, in a word, whatever is of our own doing. Not within our power are our body, our property, reputation, office, and, in a word, whatever is not of our own doing."

2. **Passions and emotions** such as fear, lust, anger, envy, resentment etc **are personal choices**, regardless of outer circumstances.

This is based in Epictetus' teachings that there can be no such thing as being the 'victim' of another, you can only be a victim of your own thoughts. It's all about self-discipline.

"Keep this thought handy, when you feel a fit of rage coming on, it isn't manly to be enraged. Rather, gentleness and civility are more human, and therefore manlier. A real man doesn't give way to anger and discontent, and such a person has strength, courage and endurance unlike the angry and complaining. The nearer a man comes to a calm mind, the closer he is to strength."
- Marcus Aurelius, Meditations, 11.1.5b

In other words, anger is weakness of will. Are you going to be a puppet of your anger or appetite? Just because someone calls you a name, does that mean you have to jump? Just because your anger says 'jump', do you have to jump? Not if you are the master of your destiny.

"Frame your thoughts like this - you are a mature person, you won't let yourself be enslaved by this any longer, no longer pulled like a puppet by every impulse, and you'll stop complaining about your present fortune or dreading the future."   *- Marcus Aurelius, Meditations, 2.2*

3. **Awareness/Assessment of Self and of Circumstances**

"Above all, it is necessary for a person to have a true self-estimate for we commonly think that we can do more than we really can."
- Seneca, On Tranquility of the Mind, 5.2

How can you really be considered self-aware if you refuse to consider your weaknesses, patterns and instincts? Are you ready to have that "hard-talk" with yourself? Be careful of dangerous overestimation of yourself or of situations. Understand that awareness is freedom.

"The person is free who lives as they wish, neither compelled, not hindered, nor limited - whose choices aren't hampered, whose desires succeed, and who doesn't fall into what repels them. Who wishes to live in deception, tripped up, mistaken, undisciplined, complaining, in a rut? No one. These are base people who don't live as they wish; and so, no base person is free." - Epictetus, Discourses, 4.1.1-3a

In Greek, the word, *'Oiesis'*, self-deception and *'Hybris'*, hubris, are seen as dangerous traps that we set for ourselves. We must exercise self-awareness at all times, otherwise, we may have a *tragic* end, like the hero *Oedipus*.

"Zeno would say that nothing is more hostile to a firm grasp on knowledge than self-deception." - Diogenes Laertius, Lives of the Eminent Philosophers, 7.23

4. Objective, Free Thinking

Don't get caught up in all the drama and other illusions of the ego. Be careful not to allow toxic thoughts to slip in, by being constantly vigilant.

"Your mind will take the shape of what you frequently hold in thought, for the human spirit is colored by such impressions." -Marcus Aurelius, Meditations 5.16

"Drama, combat, terror, numbness, and subservience, every day these things wipe out your sacred principles, whenever your mind entertains them uncritically, or lets them slip in." -Marcus Aurelius, Meditations, 10.9

"Hold sacred your capacity for understanding. For in it is our ruling principle that won't allow anything to enter that

is neither inconsistent with nature nor with the constitution of a logical creature. It's what demands due diligence, care for others, and obedience to God."

-Marcus Aurelius, Meditations, 3.9

The Discipline of Desire

1. **Cultivate** Fortitude and Resilience through **positive habits**, because *"We are what we repeatedly do"*, as Aristotle taught.

   Stoics believed that it is great to be inspired, from time to time, but real transformation happens in small, consistent steps that work, such as waking up early in the morning, making our bed each day, meditating, journalling, fasting regularly etc. Because a strong soul is better than good luck.

   > *"We must undergo a hard winter training and not rush into things for which we haven't prepared."*
   > *-Epictetus, Discourses, 1.2.32*

   > *"The rational soul is stronger than any kind of fortune - from its own share, it guides its affairs here or there, and is itself the cause of a happy or miserable life."*
   > *-Seneca, Moral Letters, 98.2b*

2. **Live with Kindness and Virtue;** it will make you invincible.

   > *"Kindness is invincible, but only when it's sincere, with no hypocrisy or faking."*
   > *-Marcus Aurelius, Meditations, 11.18.5.9a*

   The Stoics studied Plato and Socrates who taught that the real secret to philosophy is learning to love.

   > *"Dig deep within yourself, for there is a fountain of goodness ever ready to flow if you will keep digging."*
   > *-Marcus Aurelius, Meditations, 7.59*

   > *"The wise person can lose nothing. Such a person has everything stored up for themselves, leaving nothing to*

111

Fortune, their own goods are held firm, bound in virtue,
which requires nothing from chance, and therefore can't be
either increased or diminished."

-Seneca, On the Firmness of the Wise, 5.4

3. **'Amor Fati'** is about accepting your fate.

When something happens that we dreaded would happen, what is
more intelligent to dwell on: Wishing that it hadn't happened or
figuring out what to do about it, and possibly even benefitting
from the event?

This premise, that we don't control what happens to us but we _do_
control how we respond to what happens to us, is expressed in
this quote from Marcus Aurelius:

> *"The impediment to action advances action,*
> *what stands in the way becomes the way."*

In this way, there is no such thing as a setback or a problem or an
obstacle. There's simply an opportunity to try a different strategy.
It may not be what we thought, or were expecting, but it's what
we need to do. Perhaps it's not what we would have preferred,
but still good enough to work with. Obstacles feed our
determination to succeed, like gasoline feeds the fire. This is what
the Stoics call, *"Amor Fati"* ie love of one's fate. There is a
belief that difficulties can bring out the best in us:

> *"Igne natura renovatur integra."*
> *(Motto in Latin: Through fire, nature is reborn whole.)*

Throughout history great men and women have responded to
problems, obstacles and adversity in a similar way :

> *"Don't seek for everything to happen as you wish it would,*
> *but rather wish that everything happens as it actually will -*
> *then your life will flow well." -Epictetus, Enchiridion, 8*

Some people mistake Amor Fati for being fatalistic, leading to
non-action. On the contrary, it's about accepting what has

happened and using the time to re-group resources, in order to proceed to the next steps. It is, in fact, the only useful and practical thing you can do. Everything else is a waste of time and energy.

4. Meditation on Mortality 'Memento Mori'

The literal translation of this is 'Remembering you will die.`` Stoics meditate daily on their mortality to revive their commitment to a principle centered life, to be more grateful and free from being anxious.

Imagine a soldier who is leaving for duty tomorrow, not knowing whether they'll return or not. How would they behave and see things? Firstly, they'll get their affairs in order. They will handle their business. They will tell their family and children how much they love them. They wouldn't have time for quarrelling or petty matters. In the morning they are prepared to go, hoping for the best, but knowing that they might not come back.

> *"Let us prepare our minds as if we'd come to the very end of life. Let us postpone nothing. Let us balance life's books each day... The one who puts the finishing touches on their life each day is never short of time."*
> *-Seneca, Moral Letters, 102.7b-8a*

The Discipline of Action

1. Stoics live according to the **cardinal values** that lead to Virtue and Eudaimonia; Experience has proven that when wealth and power are targeted for their own sake, it leads to a feeling of emptiness.

> *"How much better it is to be known for doing well by many than for living extravagantly? How much more worthy than spending on sticks and stones is it to spend on people?"*
> *-Musonius Rufus, Lectures, 19.91.26-28*

Stoics believe that their virtue and honor are the greatest treasure and they would not 'sell out' at least not as readily as people with low moral standards. This moral backbone makes them unshakable in the most challenging circumstances.

2. Solving Problems through a **View From Above**

When we see the bigger picture, we can more easily find solutions and things begin to 'click'. A great idea can come from this raised perspective.

> *"How beautifully Plato put it. Whenever you want to talk about people, it's best to take a bird's eye-view and see everything all at once - of gatherings, armies, farms, weddings and divorces, births and deaths, noisy courtrooms or silent spaces, every foreign people, holidays, memorials, markets - all blended together and arranged in a pairing of opposites."*   -Marcus Aurelius, Meditations, 7.48

Marcus Aurelius told himself: *"Many of the anxieties that harass you are superfluous... Expand into an ampler region, letting your thoughts sweep over the entire universe."*

3. **Do your duty.**

> *"Never shirk the proper dispatch of your duty, no matter if you are freezing or hot, groggy or well, rested, vilified or praised, not even if dying or pressured by other demands. Even dying is one of the important assignments of life and, in this as in all else, make the most of your resources to do well in the duty at hand."*
>   -Marcus Aurelious, Meditations, 6.2

The Stoics believed that every person, animal and thing has a purpose or a place in nature. Think of a symphony orchestra. Each musician has their role to play in the Grand Plan of Nature.

> *"On those mornings when you struggle with getting up, keep this thought in mind - I am awakening to the work of a human being. Why then am I annoyed that I am going to do*

what I am made for, the very things for which I was put into this world? Or was I made for this, to snuggle under the covers and keep warm? It's so pleasurable. Were you then made for pleasure? In short, to be coddled, or to exert yourself?"   *-Marcus Aurelius, Meditations, 5.1*

4. **Be Pragmatic**.

"That cucumber is bitter, so toss it out! There are thorns on the path, then keep away! Enough said. Why ponder the existence of nuisance? Such thinking would make you a laughing-stock to the true student of Nature, just as a carpenter or cobbler would laugh if you pointed out the sawdust and chips on the floors of their shops. Yet while those shopkeepers have dustbins for disposal, Nature has no need of them..."   *-Marcus Aurelius, Meditations, 8.50*

So in other words, don't wait for perfection or utopia, be pragmatic and make the best of it. There's always more room to maneuver and negotiate than you think. As Seneca wrote,

"Apply yourself to thinking through difficulties - hard times can be softened, tight squeezes widened, and heavy loads made lighter for those who can apply the right pressure." *(On Tranquility of Mind, 10.4b)*

Stoicism is a clear path for entrepreneurship, for personal happiness, for navigating a world that is inherently unpredictable. It's a philosophy for self-made individuals, for resilient and robust individuals, for resourceful people who understand that they don't control outside forces, but they can control their internal ones.

Inspired by Socrates, who lived and died by his values, the Stoics are not prepared to 'sell-out' what they value most; *Tranquility, fearlessness and freedom. As Epictetus explains, so simply.*

"What is the fruit of these teachings? Only the most beautiful and proper harvest of the truly educated - tranquility, fearlessness and freedom. We should not trust the masses who say only the free can be educated, but rather

the lovers of wisdom who say that only the educated are free."

The correct approach of practicing Stoicism

Although Stoicism provides an excellent philosophy for navigating through life, it should not be confused with self-repression or denial and should not be the only method employed when the problems are overwhelming or arising out of physical conditions.

A Stoic should seek the support and advice of family, friends and professionals if the situation requires it. Seeking help isn't a sign of weakness. It's a display of wisdom.

> *"Don't be ashamed of needing help. You have a duty to fulfill just like a soldier on the wall of battle. So what if you are injured and can't climb up without another soldier's help?" - Marcus Aurelius*

SECTION 4
Scientific Foundations

The Scientific Foundations

Science has advanced a lot since the time of the ancient philosophers and has added a great deal of knowledge to the matters they explored. The amazing thing though, is that the basic insights they developed back then are still valid, relevant and widely applied today.

The reason for this, is that no matter how much our knowledge and technology have advanced, we still have to deal with the same basic issues - unhealthy emotions like excessive fear, frustration, anger and anxiety, as well as our quest for happiness and eudaimonia.

The uniqueness of The ALKISTIS Method® is that it effectively integrates modern scientific, evidence-based techniques such as neurocoaching, Cognitive-Behavioral Therapy (CBT), etc., with the ageless wisdom of ancient Greek philosophy for achieving optimum results.

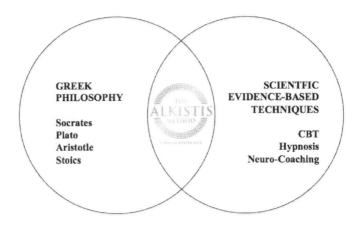

Scientific & Evidence Based Techniques

Scientific research by leading institutions like Harvard and M.I.T., have since made startling discoveries about the human brain, especially in recent decades. Some of these insights can help leaders and ordinary people dramatically improve employee morale, productivity, and retention. An important result of this research was the development of *neurocoaching*, a fusion of applied neuroscience, performance psychology and neurolinguistics. It gives emphasis to neurology and engaging the whole nervous system to get the desired results, by using neurological or 'embodied thinking' processes, rather than the advice style model.

The benefits and potential of neurocoaching cannot be overstated. If self-leadership and eudaimonia is our goal, this approach can offer us our basic techniques for successfully reaching it.

In this section we will get a brief overview of some of the advances that have brought us to a modern approach for optimizing human performance.

We will also see that *these techniques fall perfectly in line with the insights and teachings of the ancient philosophers*, for the simple reason that we, as people, our problems and desires, haven't changed since then.

Behaviourism and Pavlov's Dogs

Behaviourism is the theory that behaviour can be explained in terms of conditioning, without appeal to thoughts or feelings, and that psychological disorders are best treated by altering behaviour patterns.

The origins of this theory lie with Ivan Pavlov, the first Russian Nobel laureate, who is best known for his famous 1901 experiment, usually referred to as "Pavlov's Dogs", in which he developed the concept of the "Conditioned Reflex".

The experiment showed that when a buzzer sounded simultaneously as food was presented to a dog, the dog *connects* the sound of the stimulus (buzzer) with the presentation of the food, and began to salivate even if the food was not present.

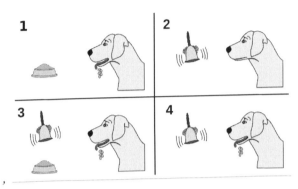

Image (CC) 2.0: The famous experiment of Nobel Prize Winner, Dr.Ivan Pavlov

His research caused a revolution in training, learning and therapy approaches. The idea of 'conditioning' as a form of (automatic) learning and training for humans, became the basis of what we know as modern *Behaviorism*, a new psychology based on training new, positive, desired behaviors, sometimes in a matter of minutes rather than through many years of psychoanalysis.

The truth is that all of us have been trained in certain ways, with limiting beliefs and patterns of behaviour, a bit like circus animals. In the circus, for example, a trainer will tie a young elephant's foot to a post, with a cord and each time the little elephant tries to walk away, it gets painful cuts by the chord. Over time, it develops the deep belief that it should not, and cannot break free and it gives up. Thereafter, *even when the cord is removed, the elephant continues acting as if it still existed.*

Much in a similar way, as little kids, growing up, our family and the specific culture that we were surrounded by gave us clear signals and punished us when we did something they did not agree with. Slowly, we became 'programmed' unconsciously to act like them and talk like them, and think like them.

So, now as conscious adults who want to take charge of our life, we must become mindful and selective. We need to ask ourselves which of those beliefs that we learned earlier on in our life or our career, are no longer useful.

The *"A-Ha!"* realization is that *"YES"*, we *can* be re-trained in new behaviors *regardless of our age*. It does not, and *need not* require years and years of therapy to change our limiting thoughts and behaviours so we can take control of our lives. The brain is simple to reprogram when there is a will to do so.

Just because something is simple and straightforward though, does not make it less powerful or effective. This evidence-based knowledge is being applied in all sorts of fields where a new stimulus will cause a whole new, improved response in people: It's like we can *just flip a switch (on-off)* in our mind, for new, excellent, extraordinary results.

This natural healing system that each one of us is born with, which allows our brains to overcome our phobias and traumas by '*flipping*

a switch' to a new thought/stimulus, is a very important tool in taking charge of ourselves.

It allows us to reprogram our minds and through continuous application, change the way our mind works and the way it perceives ourself and the world.

This is something the ancient philosophers knew very well, and applied in practice. As Aristotle famously said:

> *"We are what we repeatedly do ...*
> *Excellence is therefore a habit."*

 Note: If you are interested in a medallion for experimenting with "pressing a button" to alter your state, please follow this link:

www.alkistis.net/medallion.html

Cognitive Behavioral Therapy

Albert Ellis was an American psychologist who in 1955 set forth the first cognitive-behavioral therapy, the 'Rational Emotive Behavioral Therapy' (REBT), in which he proposed that emotional and behavioral problems could be relieved through a process of cognitive restructuring or, put more simply, *the changing of faulty thoughts and beliefs through examination and understanding*. This treatment model represented a major shift from the dominant treatment model of the day, Freudian psychoanalysis, which emphasized the bringing forward of subconscious thoughts as a way of changing behavior.

Ellis got his ideas from an old and trusted source - the ancient Greek philosophers, and more specifically from Socrates' Maieutic method of inquiry (which we discuss in the chapter on Socrates, in Section 3) and Aristotle's notion of *Prohairesis*.

Prohairesis (Ancient Greek: προαίρεσις; variously translated as "moral character", "will", "volition", "choice", "intention", or "moral choice") represents the choice involved in giving or withholding assent to impressions, in other words, the choice we have on how we interpret things. The use of this Greek word was first introduced into philosophy by Aristotle in the Nicomachean Ethics. It is what distinguishes human beings from all other creatures.

According to Aristotle (and later Epictetus), nothing can be considered either good, or bad, aside from those things that are within our own power to control, and the only thing fully in our power to control is our own volition (prohairesis) which forms our impressions. By exerting their prohairesis (will, volition, or choice), people can choose rationally their impression of an event and how to deal with it.

"Between stimulus and response there is a space. In that space is our power to choose our response. In our response lies our growth and our freedom." - Dr. Viktor Frankl

In the 1960s, another psychologist, Aaron Beck, identified fifteen specific ways in which our beliefs can drift away from reality and cause depression, anxiety, and other difficulties. He called these cognitive distortions, and he, too, believed that re-aligning one's cognition with reality would reduce suffering. His work was similarly built on the framework of the Greek philosophers.

Cognitive behavioral therapy (CBT) is a psychosocial intervention that is the most widely used evidence-based practice for improving mental health. Guided by empirical research, CBT focuses on the development of personal coping strategies that aim at solving current problems and changing unhelpful patterns in cognitions (e.g. thoughts, attitudes or beliefs), behaviors, and regulating emotions. Though it was originally designed to treat depression, it is now being successfully used for many mental health conditions, but also for leadership training.

The CBT model is based on a combination of the basic principles from behavioral and cognitive psychology. It differs from historical approaches to psychotherapy, such as psychoanalysis, where the therapist formulates a diagnosis based on looking for the unconscious meaning behind behaviors. Cognitive Behavioral therapy focuses on the *actual behavior* or problem caused by a diagnosed mental disorder, not the disorder itself. The role of the therapist is to support the client in finding and practising effective strategies to decrease the *symptoms* of the disorder.

Primary characteristics which distinguish CBT from other forms of therapy can be summed up with the following points:

- The focus is on the current problem instead of its historical influences.
- Emphasis is on using evident behaviour changes, to determine progress.
- Treatment is clearly specific.

Stress & Coping Research

There's a large body of research on mechanisms of psychological stress and coping strategies known as the "stress and coping" literature. Richard Lazarus' seminal cognitive appraisal model of stress and coping provided the basis for the cognitive model of emotions employed in most CBT. This theory states that the amount of stress experienced is proportionate to the extent by which the perceived demands (or level of threat) in a situation outweighs your perceived ability to cope with it (or control the outcome).

This leads to the "goodness of fit hypothesis" (GOFH), proposed by Lazarus and Folkman (1984), which states that healthy coping consists of matching our coping style to the level of control we have over problems in daily life. In other words, the hypothesis says that people will suffer less stress if, on the one hand, they accept events appraised as *beyond* their control, employing "emotion-focused" coping to reduce distress, and on the other hand they actively problem-solve events perceived as *under* their control.

This hypothesis is similar to the Stoic principle of Dichotomy of Control. In general, modern research on the "goodness of fit" hypothesis and other aspects of stress and coping is perfectly aligned with the insights of Stoicism and Greek Philosophy.

In the next section we will explore the function of the brain from a scientific perspective.

Brain User's Manual

Probably the best known model for understanding the structure of the brain, in relation to its evolutionary history is the famous *triune brain theory*, which was developed by Paul MacLean in the 1960s, which defines three levels of brain activity: The Reptilian, The Mammalian and The Neocortex.

Although this model is currently seen as an oversimplified organizing theme by some in the field of comparative neuroscience, it continues to hold public interest because of its simplicity. While technically inaccurate in some respects, it remains one of very few approximations of the truth we have to work with and is quite sufficient for our purposes.

More specifically, the three levels of brain activity, are:

The *Reptilian* Brain, the oldest of the three, which appeared over 500 million years ago in fish, and controls the body's vital functions such as heart rate, breathing, body temperature and balance. The reptilian brain is reliable but tends to be somewhat rigid, compulsive and re-active.

The *Mammalian* (or limbic) Brain, which appeared over 150 million years ago and can record memories of behaviours that produced agreeable and disagreeable experiences, so it is responsible for what are called emotions in human beings. The main structures of the limbic brain are the hippocampus, the amygdala, and the hypothalamus. The mammalian brain is the seat of the value judgments that we make, often unconsciously, that exert such a strong influence on our behaviour.

The *Neocortex* first assumed importance in primates only 2-3 million years ago, and with its two large cerebral hemispheres has culminated into what we have come to recognize as the human

125

brain. These two hemispheres have been responsible for the development of human language, abstract thought, imagination, and conscious, strategic thinking.

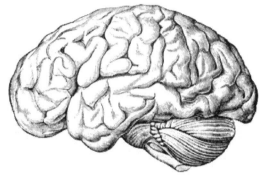

Image (CC) 2.0: A drawing of the human brain.

These three parts of the brain do not operate independently of one another. They have established neural pathways of interconnections through which they influence one another.

One of the problems we have as humans, is that most people allow their *reptilian or mammalian brain to make decisions for them*, especially when we feel threatened, instead of applying the neocortex, the most recently evolved section of the brain.

The reptilian brain functions based on "fight-or-flight" reactions. Just imagine how a reptile, such as a lizard reacts when it is feeling threatened. It will either 'fight' which means it will attack, or it will take 'flight', which means that it will "run off" from the scene, as fast as it can. Both of these activities need ample injections of adrenaline.

People who have anger management problems, who often 'attack' others either physically or verbally have allowed their reptilian brain to 'hijack' their thinking; The adrenaline injections, 'block' the functions of the 'neocortex', reducing their capacity for rational thought.

People who allow their mammalian brain to do their thinking for them will always be at a loss, if they do not step-back and question their beliefs before getting caught up in a self-created 'melodrama', and creating arguments based on false beliefs and distortions that are not true or valid.

Let us take a moment of self-reflection: When was the last time your reptilian brain 'hijacked' your mind and you lost your temper? Notice the results when you allow that to happen? What sort of person do you become? Who would you be without that anger/frustration/ego? Who could you be, if you allowed your mind to work at full capacity, as Aristotle would say, with Areté?

Neuroscience tells us that the brain can constantly learn, our whole life long, and that we can acquire new, more useful beliefs that will get us to where we want to go from now on. Here is where the neocortex of our brain comes in.

The neocortex is the part of our brain, capable of conscious self-reflection, imagination and metacognition (thinking about our thinking processes). Metacognition is also a very important part of *Prosoche* ie *observing, organizing and managing your thoughts and energy*.

It is the most evolved and most recent 'updated software' of our brain. It is also the seat of Ethos, and 'higher-level' thinking, such as visualization and strategizing. It is solutions-oriented and not fear-based like the reptilian brain. The neocortex offers a new inner freedom to those who use it.

Rewiring your Brain

From Fear, Frustration and Anxiety to Calm, Confidence and Self-leadership.

People spend the majority of their life living under stress. Stress is when your body's knocked out of 'order' (*homeostasis*); the stress response is what your body innately does to return itself back to 'order'. That's the first definition of *resilience* .

There are three types of stress. *Physical stress* is from an injury, an accidental fall or trauma, *Chemical stress* from viruses, bacteria, blood sugar levels, heavy metals, hormones, foods and hangovers, and *emotional stress* like traffic jams, internet disconnections, second mortgages, single parenting and your doing your taxes.

Each one of those things knocks your brain and body out of balance, so all organisms in nature have evolved to tolerate short-term stress. For example, if a deer is chased by a pack of wolves and escapes, fifteen minutes later it goes back to grazing, and its stress is over.

Human beings are different though, in that *we can turn on the stress response just by thought* alone. You can begin to think about some future worst-case scenario and because the privilege of human beings is that *we can make thought more real than anything else*, we can focus on that fear-thought *to the exclusion of everything else,* and *we* can knock our body out of physiological balance (*homeostasis*) just by thought alone.

Our unconscious mind *believes it is actually in* that experience in the present moment. Or on other occasions we focus on past bitter memories that are 'written' in the recesses of our brain and like magic, we bring them to life through dwelling on those old traumas, and *in that moment it is real.* The hormones of stress push the genetic buttons that create disease. No organism can tolerate living in emergency mode for extended periods of time without it eventually becoming sickness. So if you can *turn on* the stress response just by thought alone, and we know that the hormones of stress regulate genes that *create* disease, it's easy to conclude that your thoughts can make you well too.

The hormones of stress give the body and brain a rush of energy (mainly adrenaline) and it's *like a narcotic.* It becomes a drug and people become very addicted to the adrenaline and other stress hormones. They use the problems and conditions in their life to *reaffirm* their emotional addiction so they can reaffirm who they think they are; ie the bad relationship, the bad job, the terrible circumstances, all of that is in place because the person needs to reaffirm their emotional addiction. So then if you become addicted to your own chemicals through (illusory) thoughts, when it comes time to change them, *just like an addict,* you will try to *stop* the new, positive thoughts from coming into your mind.

Let us say, you have been having insecure thoughts for the past twenty or thirty years. It is going to feel very *familiar,* even comfortable. "I am insecure" will be a 'normal' thought for you. Whenever you say "I AM…. (anything)" what you are saying is that you are commanding your mind and body towards a certain result / *Telos*/ destiny / outcome.

The moment you decide you are no longer going to think insecure thoughts, your body is going to look back up at your brain and say *"Hey! I modified my receptor sites for you so many years ago, we've been doing this for twenty years… I'm counting on those chemicals coming… and now you're telling me that we are just going to stop this 'routine'?"* It will start sending signals back to the brain *to make the same choice* as you have been making for so long! If you keep that period going on for weeks or months it's called *a temperament or a personality trait:* He has a bad temper, she gets hysterical, he throws tantrums easily, she has anger management issues, etc…

So your twenty years of hatred, bitterness, anger or your fifteen years of fear and insecurity is the very reason that you get sick, or feel exhausted, or you've lost your enthusiasm for life. "Why are you so angry?" people ask. "Well this experience happened to me nine years ago…" An article in Scientific American recently claimed that *scientists have found that 50% of what you say about your past is not true.* We make up stuff in our head, looking to reaffirm that we are "right". Remember Plato's Cave Allegory? It is amazing how much people distort things in their mind.

Living by those same familiar emotions means that nothing new is happening in our life, so we feel safe, because we are at least *alive* ie. we have survived another day on Earth. The body literally is *living in the past* and we can not create a new future holding on to the emotions of the past. We are basically trying to predict the future from the past. That's called *anxiety, neurosis and insomnia.* We're missing out on the possibility to be grateful, the possibility to be in wonder, to feel really alive, the possibility to feel at peace and fulfilled.

Most people have to hit a point of crisis where they finally start taking their attention off their outer world and start to ask themselves some bigger (self-reflective, philosophical) questions: *Who amI ? What is a greater expression of myself? What would I have to change to be happy? What do I really want after all? Who in history do I admire that I want to be like?* They begin to contemplate and speculate and rehearse *who they could become.* Actually, the mere process of thinking about who we can become, begins to change our brain. (See also image below on neurogenesis.)

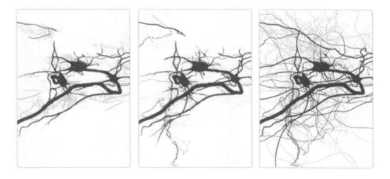

Image (CC) 2.0:I Neurogenesis - growth of new neural connections.

When you combine a clear intention with an elevated emotion that's heartfelt, you move into a new state of being. You can begin to remind yourself every single day of who you want to be. Through regular practices, like meditation, you begin to *cause your brain to fire in new sequences and new patterns* and new combinations and you make your brain work differently. According to neuroscience your brain begins to fire and create new circuits. You are essentially rewiring your brain.

"We become what we repeatedly do." - Aristotle

When you are asking open-ended questions, the frontal brain lobe, *like a great symphony leader,* looks out of the landscape of the entire brain and begins to select different networks of neurons and seamlessly pieces them together to create a new mind. The moment the brain begins to fire in tandem, the frontal lobe creates a picture. That picture is called *an intention* and *when you can make that picture more real than anything else and you begin to feel inspired by it,* and your body's *no longer living in the past,* you begin a new state of being, with new values and actions. This creates a new reality.

The more we practice a new state, the more it becomes the default setting. *Scientific studies have shown* that it takes *as little as sixty-six days* to take on a new habit. Many *Askesis* in The ALKISTIS Method® aim to create new habits and new default settings, for new outcomes.

Try this practice, called "Prohairesis":

The next time you have an urge to get angry, to grab a cigarette, to gobble a cupcake, to waste your precious working time on social media, (or any other negative habit), wait about ten minutes or count to 500 before you do it; Say to yourself in a loving way (never mean), "I will allow you to get angry, I will allow you to smoke, I will allow you to grab that cupcake, I will allow you to interrupt your work on this important project to scan Facebook, but in ten minutes from now. If you still have that urge to do so, I will allow it."

Note: Some (mistaken) theories say to count to ten backwards and then do it, but scientific studies show that it takes ten minutes for this 'wave of desire' to pass. (*For more on this, a good book is, Indistractable: How to Control Your Attention and Choose Your Life, by Nir Eyal.*)

Hypno-Learning and Meditation in Alpha State

The use of hypnosis and meditation has been scientifically proven to be an effective tool to increase memory, mindfulness and to reprogram our brain for new habits.

This was well known to the ancient philosophers like Plato and Aristotle, who gave a great deal of attention to the relationship between the soul and the body. The schools that they founded incorporated vigorous physical and musical training.

Deep relaxation practices of consciously recognizing and controlling our thoughts and dreams, has been around for centuries. Since ancient Greek times, "Morpheus" the Greek god of Dreams was venerated. Aristotle, the Greek philosopher and scientist, (384-322 BC) who wrote about this practice in his works, ('On Dreaming' and 'On Sleep and Waking') was the first to note that the images and symbols we see in dream and myth speak directly to our subconscious. Hippocrates, (460-377BC) the Father of modern Medicine, praised induced dreaming & hypnosis for its benefits.

Now, thousands of years later, science is proving how much our physical state affects our mental and emotional state, and how we can 'manipulate' our physiology to develop our full potential.

Doctors recommend daily practice of a deeply relaxing inner state, to help us manage stress and anxiety. Scientific Studies have proven that in a relaxed state, the mind is more than 200% more receptive to suggestions, than in an ordinary, conscious state. In addition, when we introduce a 'positive mission statement' during this practice, it can bring on positive powerful changes in our life.

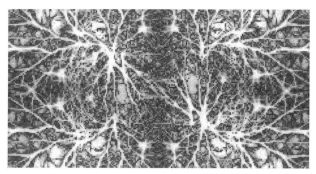

Image (CC) 2.0 : Neural networks, 'firing' electrical pulses to each other.

At the root of all our thoughts, emotions and behaviours is the communication between neurons within our brains. Brainwaves are produced by synchronised electrical pulses from masses of neurons communicating with each other.

Our brainwaves change according to what we're doing and feeling. The higher frequencies are dominant when we feel hyper-alert. When slower brain waves are dominant, as in hypnosis, we can feel relaxed, slow, dreamy and open to suggestions or instructions. In Meditative (*Alpha*) and Deeply Relaxed (*Theta*) states, the mind becomes a receiver, much like a radio or television, tuning into a specific 'Learning Channel'. (Greek Hypnagogia, Hypnos = sleep Agogia = learning).

The benefits of hypnosis, hypno-learning, meditation and hypnotherapy for learning new, constructive thinking habits and overcoming negative habits are discussed in the Askesis "Morpheas Mind Mechanics", in Section 2, with the use of a "Deep Relaxation through Guided Visualization" audio mp3.

Researchers have long known that sleeping plays an important role in the learning process. While we are in a deeply relaxed state (Alpha, Theta), our brains are busy organizing and consolidating the information and events we encountered that day. Important things get filed away, while the rest gets deleted to make room for new learning. A new study from the Decoding Sleep Interfaculty Research Cooperation at the University of Bern, Switzerland, has shown that the brain's channels for learning are open during sleep.

"What we found in our study is that the sleeping brain can actually encode new information and store it for long term. Even more, the sleeping brain is able to make new associations," said Marc Züst, co-author of the study.

The hypnagogic state It:

- Calms your nerves and helps you handle stress better in general.
- Cultivates the process of self-induced deep relaxation, so that you can 'relax yourself' *at will*.
- Increases your mindfulness, allowing you to become more intuitive.
- Offers space to insert deeply empowering *positive affirmations* for personal transformation.
- Relieves migraines and other psychosomatic stress related symptoms.

Brain Waves Chart

| | Beta Waves | Frequency: 12 to 30 Hz |
| Alert | | |

| | Alpha Waves | Frequency: 7.5 to 12 Hz |
| Meditative | | |

| | Theta Waves | Frequency: 4 to 7.5 Hz |
| Deeply Relaxed | | |

| | Delta Waves | Frequency: up to 4 Hz |
| Sleeping | | |

depth of mind

The ALKISTIS Method® practitioners apply hypno-learning and meditation techniques for overcoming limiting habits and reprogramming our brain for outstanding performance. In order to take charge of our life, we should start by taking charge of the 'automatic' programs running in 'robot-mode' since we were young.

You can download the free guided meditation (mp3 format) from: www.alkistis.net/free_mp3.html

"People don't know that a third of their life is a third where they could change or structure or better themselves," writes Adam Horowitz, PhD at MIT

"Whether you're talking about memory augmentation or creativity augmentation or improving mood the next day or improving test performance, there's all these things you can do at night that are practically important," Horowitz added in an interview with OneZero of Medium.com

Epilogue

"Memento Mori" The Ultimate Key To Inner Freedom?

"Let us prepare our minds as if we'd come to the very end of life. Let us postpone nothing. Let us balance life's books each day. ... The one who puts the finishing touches on their life each day is never short of time." - Seneca

Each person's life, is an "odyssey", an adventure, a journey. Your life will have its ups and downs, and then it will all come to an end someday over the horizon. Just look around in nature and you will be reminded.

"Memento Mori" ie the practice of meditating on the inevitability of death and the transience of life, was common amongst Greek and later Roman philosophers. In one of the most illuminating passages, *The Meditations*, Marcus Aurelius asserts the Stoic and Socratic view that *true philosophy is mainly in "waiting for death with good grace."* (Meditations, 2.17).

To modern people like you and I, this may sound like an awful idea. Who wants to think about their death?

But what if we stopped being afraid of it and instead embraced this truth, and took charge of it. What if meditating on death was the 'Ultimate Key' to living life to the fullest and to our freedom?

In Plato's renowned dialogue in his work *Phaedo*, he describes how composed Socrates was in his final hours. *"Although I was witnessing the death of one who was my friend, I had no feeling of pity, for the man appeared happy both in manner and words as he died nobly and without fear."* (Phaedo, 58e)

Xenophon writes that Socrates, faced his death-sentence by the court with absolute serenity and fortitude, and that it *was "generally agreed that no one in the memory of man has ever met his death more nobly."* (Memorabilia, 4.8).

In this book you have been offered *The Askesis* and a wealth of information inspired by some of the greatest minds in all of history, to make the best of yourself and your life.

The Greek philosophers advised that it is wise to meditate each evening on being grateful for our life and awaken every morning planning our day as if it were *on, or very near* the last day of our life. The reason is that this "view from above", the greater picture of our life, can liberate us from pettiness and self-created drama. It is a way of focusing on the "here and now" and this is the irony: By contemplating on our own death, we can intensify our appreciation of our life. Hence the motto, *"Seize The Day"* from (Latin) *Carpe Diem* and (Greek) ἄδραξε την ημέρα.

In today's fast paced, greed driven society, where people experience deep levels of anxiety and having 'lost religion' to science, there is a real *vacuum* which Greco-Roman Philosophy can help fill. In recent years it is experiencing a rebirth, through a movement called *"Modern Stoicism"*. Many famous people have espoused it from Nelson Mandela, Bill Clinton, Arnold Schwarzenegger, Victor Frankl, Bill Gates, Warren Buffet to Nassim Nicholas Taleb. It is not by chance that Steve Jobs had once said, *"I would give up all my technology for an afternoon with Socrates."*

Stoicism is, in a sense, the Western world's answer to Buddhism. Modern Stoicism, like Modern Humanism too, is increasingly appealing to people who:

- Want to live an ethical life informed by science and reason
- Want their philosophy to be at the same time coherent and flexible enough to adjust to new times and circumstances.

Even though over two and a half thousand years have passed, the way of Greco-Roman philosophy remains unchallenged, relevant and universal for all humans. *It is a set a values and practices, which anybody can apply and benefit from, regardless of their faith, to make them inwardly strong and free no matter how challenging a situation may be.*

Each day, a practicing philosopher clears his/her mind through reading or meditating on their values (see askesis on "Personal Mission Statement"). This daily Askesis rejuvenates and reminds us who we really are and what we are really here for. Every night before sleep, a practitioner goes over their day and identifies mistakes and feels healthy pride in worthy accomplishments. This is reminiscent of the evening self-reflection exercises taught by one of the greatest Greek philosophers, Pythagoras (c. 570 – c. 495 BC), whose "Golden Verses" teach:

> *"Do not receive sleep on your tender eyes, before you have thrice gone through each of the day's deeds: Where have I failed myself? What have I done? What duty have I not fulfilled?"*

And are these not the very same questions that we will all eventually be asking ourselves at a ripe old age, when we will be reflecting back on our life, to determine if it was well-lived? "Memento Mori" therefore, just may be the key to freedom and a fulfilling life.

Song of Seikilos

As long as you live, shine,
Have no grief at all.
For your life is short,
and time will claim its toll.

The Seikilos epitaph is the oldest surviving complete musical composition, including musical notation, from anywhere in the world. The epitaph has been variously dated, but seems to be either from the 1st or the 2nd century AD.

See Youtube video: Ancient Greece: Song of Seikilos

Links to Lifelong Learning

"Gyrasko diae pola didaskomenos" (**Greek:** γηράσκω δ' αἰεὶ πολλά διδασκόμενος) — *"As I grow older I keep being taught new things"* a quote by Solon the famous Athenian lawmaker (whose legal work was the basis for Roman law) showing the philosopher's way of being always inquisitive and open-minded.

I.   The ALKISTIS Method® E-Learning Course

Your personal odyssey of self-reflection begins with the basic online course led by Alkistis Agio, filled with both written and a video-explanations of each *Askesis*. On-demand lecture videos, practical exercises, discussion forum, real-world homework assignments and self-reflection practices.

http://www.alkistis.net/e_learning.html

II.   Exclusive Seminars In Greece with Dr. Alkistis Agio.

If you liked reading this introduction to The ALKISTIS Method®, but you would like to do the *Askesis* in Greece and participate in one of the exclusive quarterly retreats in Greece for up to 12 participants at a time.

www.alkistis.net/groups-greece.html

III. **Become A Certified Seminar Facilitator of The ALKISTIS Method®.**

Do you feel a 'calling' to help people out of their 'Prison of the Mind'? Once you have understood that your well-being is intricately related to the well-being of your fellow human beings, you are already a 'philosopher' and can answer that 'Calling'. As Plato and Socrates taught; anyone who has escaped the 'Cave' of shadows and ignorance, *has the obligation to help others escape too.* The special curriculum of The ALKISTIS Method® is the ideal tool for personal and professional development. Completing the online course or doing an introductory seminar **is a prerequisite** for application.

Enquires: **info@alkistis.net**

IV. **Follow Alkistis Agio On Facebook.**

 https://www.facebook.com/alkistisTV/

V. **Join Our Facebook Group**

For people who have read this book and want to share their experiences. Search: Fear To Freedom® Group

VI **Leadership Trainings For Your Organization.**

'The ALKISTIS Method®' is an eclectic series of seminars that have been created for you to develop competency in effective communication, self-management and human relations skills. It is based on an integration of Neuro-Linguistic Programming, Cognitive-Behavioral Methods, Neuroscience and ancient wisdom, specifically for modern managers.

Series of Eclectic Seminars for Leadership Development that can be tailored to your organization's needs.

http://www.alkistis.net/leadership-training.html

VII **VIP Coaching-Mentorship Programs**

Overcome your greatest fears and weaknesses with the exclusive, private one-to-one sessions with Dr. Alkistis Agio.

Fill out this application form:
www.alkistis.net/contact.html

A mentor is someone who will help you pose the questions, keep your focus, and avoid biases and preconceptions that may affect your thinking.

It is a very old relationship. The word "Mentor" first appeared in Homer's Odyssey, when the goddess Athena took on the appearance of an old man by that name, in order to guide young Telemachus, Odysseus's son, in his time of difficulty.

It has since evolved to mean trusted advisor, friend, teacher, coach and wise person. History offers many examples of such mentoring relationships: Socrates and Plato, Hayden and Beethoven, Freud and Jung, etc. It is a fundamental form of human development where one person invests time, energy and personal know-how in assisting the growth and ability of another person.

It is best if the mentor is someone with experience, such as a professional coach/therapist. The very act of hiring of a mentor or coach is a step in your process of becoming serious about bringing change into your life.

The ALKISTIS Method® forces you to question your beliefs, your values and your assumptions about reality. As such, a very appropriate coaching approach is the "*The Maieutic Method*", also known as *The Socratic Method*. The word is derived from the Greek word "Maia" (midwife)", in that it is similar to assisting a birth.

Maieutics holds that many important lessons and truths cannot be taught directly from an instructor to a student/client. Instead, the client must *deduce them himself,* from his or her own experience, by interacting with an instructor who will ask the appropriate questions. The mentor's job is to help his client spread his/her wings, not fly for him.

For more information on how you can hire Dr. Alkistis Agio or trained members of her team.

www.alkistis.net/programs.html

VIII 'Golden Medallion' of the The ALKISTIS Method®

Since ancient times, jewelry has been used for raising awareness and for *triggering* empowering 'states' of consciousness. The Golden Medallion is based on *Ethos, Pathos, Logos* and can be used as a mechanism or device for 'triggering' your imagination and your capacity to envision your future more clearly...

www.alkistis.net/medallion.html

Contact our head office in central Athens, Greece
for any further inquiries: info@alkistis.net

BECOME A 'Philosopher-in-Residence'

Immerse yourself in a unique Hellenic experience by exploring Greek culture, philosophy, and art while living in a beautiful 1930's historical residence in Athens.

Throughout the year, The Agiorgiti Residence accepts applicants - writers, artists, philosophers, scholars, composers, entrepreneurs, humanists and philhellenes, whose interests concern Greek heritage and culture.

Residents live in one of six themed private bedrooms (each 20-25 m2 large) and have access to shared living spaces such as the parlor, salons, dining room, bathrooms and kitchen facilities. Residents may participate for free, in most of the cultural activities taking place at the Agiorgiti Residence, like talks, symposiums, wine-tasting & ancient gastronomy events, classical/jazz music evenings and other activities, whenever they are available. More information at:

https://www.agiorgiti-residence.com/residencies.html

Bibliography for Philosophy

i)   Annas, J. (1993) The Morality of Happiness. New York and Oxford.

ii)   Arnold, E. Vernon (1911). Roman Stoicism. Cambridge: University Press

iii)   Bobzien, Susanne (1999). Determinism and Freedom in Stoic Philosophy. Oxford: Clarendon Press.

iv)   Brink, C.O. (1955). "Theophrastus and Zeno on nature and moral theory." Phronesis 1: 123–45.

v)   Brunschwig, Jacques. (1994). Papers in Hellenistic Philosophy. Cambridge, England.

vi)   Brunschwig, J. and M. Nussbaum (1993). Passions and Perceptions: Studies in the Hellenistic Philosophy of Mind. Proceedings of the Fifth Symposium Hellenisticum. Cambridge UK: Cambridge University Press.

vii)   Cooper, John M. (1999). "Eudaimonism, the Appeal to Nature, and 'Moral Duty' in Stoicism," in Reason and Emotion (Princeton: Princeton University Press)

viii)   R. Dilcher, Studies in Heraclitus (Hildesheim: Olms, 1995).

ix)   H. Granger, "Argumentation and Heraclitus' Book," Oxford Studies in Ancient Philosophy 26 (2006), 1-17.

x)   Engstrom, Stephen and Jennifer Whiting (eds.) (1996). Aristotle, Kant, and the Stoics.

xi)   Cambridge: Cambridge University Press. Epictetus. Translations of G. Long (London: Bell, 1877) and P.E. Matheson (Oxford: 1916) are best.

xii)   Fortenbaugh, William W. (ed.) (1983). On Stoic and Peripatetic Ethics: The Work of Arius Didymus. New Brunswick and London: Transaction Books.

xiii)   Gould, Josiah B. (1970). The Philosophy of Chrysippus. Albany: State University of New York Press.

xiv)   Hicks, R.D. (1911). Stoic and Epicurean. London: Longmans Green.

xv)   Kerferd, G.B. (1972). "The search for personal identity in Stoic thought." Bulletin of the John Rylands Library 55: 177–96

xvi)   Reesor, Margaret E. (1987). "Necessity and Fate in Stoic Philosophy." In Rist (1987)187-202.

xvii)   Schofield, Malcolm and Gisela Striker (eds.) (1986). The Norms of Nature.

xviii) Cambridge: Cambridge University Press. (1991). The Stoic Idea of the City. Chicago and London: The University of Chicago Press, 1991.

xix)   Striker, Gisela (1996). Essays on Hellenistic Epistemology and Ethics. Cambridge, England.

xx)   Manning, C.E. (1973). "Seneca and the Stoics on the equality of the sexes." Mnemosyne 26 (series iv): 170–7.

xxi)   More, P .E. (1923). Hellenistic Philosophies. Princeton. An excellent work, see pp. 94–171 for Epictetus.

xxii)   Murray, G. (1921). "The Stoic philosophy." Essays and Addresses. London: Allen and Unwin.

xxiii) Nock, A.D. (1959). Journal of Roman Studies 49: 1 ff. On Posidonius.

xxiv)   Nussbaum, Martha (1994). The Therapy of Desire. Princeton University Press. thought.

xxv)   Sharples, R.W. (1996). Stoics, Epicureans and Skeptics: An Introduction to Hellenistic Philosophy. London and New York: Routledge,1996.V

xxvi)   Solmsen, F. (1961). Cleanthes or Posidonius? The Basis of Stoic Physics. Amsterdam.

xxvii) Stanton, G.R. (1968).

xxviii) Watson, G. (1966). The Stoic Theory of Knowledge. Belfast.

xxix)   Wenley, R.M. (1924; 1925). Stoicism and its Influence. Boston: Marshall Jones; London: Harrap.

xxx)   Wirszubski, G. (1950). Pp. 138–53 in Libertas as a Political Ideal at Rome during the late Republic and Early Principate (Cambridge).

xxxi)   Zeller, Eduard (1892). The Stoics, Epicureans and Skeptics. London: Longmans and Green.

Bibliography for Neuro-Coaching, CBT

1) Alford, Brad A. and Beck, Aaron T. (1997) *The integrative power of cognitive therapy.* New York: The Guildford Press

2) Clark, D. A. and Beck, A. T. (2010) *Cognitive therapy of anxiety disorders: science and practice.* New York, N.Y.: Guilford Press

3) Dobson, Deborah J. G. and Dobson, Keith S. (2009) *Evidence-based practice of cognitive behavioral therapy.* London: Guilford Press.

4) Greenberger, D. and Padesky, C. A. (1995) *Mind over mood: change how you feel by changing the way you think.* London: Guilford Press.

5) Leahy, R. L. (2003) *Cognitive therapy techniques: a practitioner's guide.* London: Guilford Press.

6) Myles, P. and Shafran, R. (2015) *The CBT handbook*. London: Robinson.

7) Wells, A. (1997) *Cognitive therapy of anxiety disorders: a practice manual and conceptual guide*. Chichester: Wiley

8) Wills, F. and Sanders, D. (2013) *Cognitive behavioural therapy: foundations for practice*. 3rd ed. London: SAGE.

9) Beck, J. S. (2011) *Cognitive behavior therapy: basics and beyond*. 2nd ed. New York: Guilford.

Testimonials

Your testimonial is deeply appreciated and it will encourage others to read this book, and TAKE CHARGE of their life. Simply go to the <u>www.amazon.com</u> sales page for this book at

https://www.amazon.com/dp/1094639540

"The ALKISTIS Method provides both philosophical and practical approach to hone your skills of Self-leadership. This Method offers a full spectrum of view points, from Aristotle and his philosophical teachings in ancient Greece to best techniques in training your brain through NLP."

Raz Choudhury
CEO, SAM.AI
Artificial Intelligence
New York, USA

"I found The ALKISTIS Method to be informative, inspiring and practical. In a non-stop world, we so often don't create the time to consider why we are doing what we are doing!
The ALKISTIS Method calls up the very oldest philosophies to create some perspective, in the information age.
An extremely worthwhile read."

Lawrence Bernstein
Speechwriter to the British Royal Family
London, England

"I find The ALKISTIS Method to be enlightening and practical. There is a wealth of useful information and exercises that assist one to reflect on simple questions which we usually shy away from, forcing one to face our reality. It gives us the necessary tools to achieve an understanding of oneself and our strengths."

Katerina Ferentinos,
Wealth Management
Merrill Lynch, New York, USA

"Alkistis is a very inspiring coach and trainer."

Paul Efmorfides,
Founder of COCO-MAT, Greece

"Alkistis has a unique, enlightening perspective."

His Excellency Abdelhadi Alkhajah,
United Arab Emirates

"Studying philosophy, especially Aristotle, has taught me to think clearly; I feel that it has helped me, even more than my MBA to become a billionaire."

Reid Hoffman
Founder of LINKEDIN
Billionaire Entrepreneur
Palo Alto, California

The Self-Leadership Quiz

How well do you lead yourself? Take the quiz below to find out, so that you can *benefit much more* from everything you are about to learn in The ALKISTIS Method®.

***Instructions**: On a scale of 0-15, where 0 is "rarely" and 15 is "often" rate yourself on these characteristics:*

1. You 'check-in' with your feelings, know what's important, and get in touch with your deep source of peaceful power.

Your score (0 - 15): _____

2. You are alert about the challenges and obstacles that you (and your team) need to solve. You are clear about the outcome you want, and take charge of the responsibilities and actions.

Your score (0 - 15): _____

3. You have an overview of the direction that you are heading towards, and often visualize the fulfillment of the vision.

Your score (0 - 15): _____

4. You are able to connect your talents and abilities to the requirements, setting targets, and aligning your thoughts and actions to your personal mission statement.

Your score (0 - 15): _____

5. You have a 'roadmap to success' with the important milestones and you make a realistic assessment of the resources available, while setting realistic standards of performance.

Your score (0 - 15): _____

6. You cultivate a support network and team, inspiring them with your vision that will benefit everyone.

Your score (0 - 15): _____

7. You motivate yourself and find meaning on a daily basis, rewarding your achievements and progress, however small.

Your score (0 - 15): _____

8. You are grateful for each moment, focusing on the positive, you immerse yourself in the 'flow of creation' sometimes losing track of time.

Your score (0 - 15): _____

9. You maintain a positive attitude, adapting to situations as they arise, accepting that 'it's never going to be perfect', but still doing your best every step of the way.

Your score (0 - 15): _____

10. You view problems as opportunities in disguise and rise to the challenges, bypassing obstacles with solutions and taking massive action.

Your score (0 - 15): _____

11. You are focused and compelled forward, as you follow what brings happiness, fulfillment and abundance for you and other stakeholders.

Your score (0 - 15): _____

Now, **add up your score** and read the analysis on the next page:

Total: _____

Congratulations for taking action!

This is the analysis of your scores:

145-165 **"Gifted"** You are gifted in terms of leading yourself, and now you can take that gift and improve how you are leading others, and yourself; The ALKISTIS Method® will empower you to TAKE CHARGE.

110-144 **"Promising"** You show a satisfactory level of self-leadership, and as you focus on improving, you can move towards having *outstanding* results; The ALKISTIS Method® will empower you to TAKE CHARGE.

75-109 **"Inconsistent"** You show some signs of self-leadership, but you need to put in much more effort to express your dormant potential; The ALKISTIS Method® will empower you to TAKE CHARGE.

35-74 **"Unsatisfactory"** Although you have self-leadership skills, you need to take your personal development much more seriously. You can make leaps if you decide you want to; The ALKISTIS Method® will empower you to TAKE CHARGE.

0-34 **"Failing"** Are you *sure* that you want to be a leader? You may have what it takes down-deep inside, but you really need to get a lot more focused and committed to your goals and personal development, which, thankfully, The ALKISTIS Method® will empower you to TAKE CHARGE.

About The Author

"My life's mission is inspiring professionals, to live up to their full potential by living according to timeless Hellenic values."

Dr. Alkistis Agio is a TEDx speaker, author and consultant with over twenty years experience in working with professionals to transform fear, frustration, anger and anxiety into calm, confident self-leadership, through her proven method, "The ALKISTIS Method®". Of Greek origin, she grew up in Montreal and has worked in Italy, France, Germany, Greece, the United States and the United Arab Emirates. She speaks five languages. Alkistis Agio studied International Banking at the Chartered Institute of Bankers in London, and later got a Master's in Integrative Psychotherapy and a Phd in Transpersonal Counseling. She has studied Neurocoaching and has served as a trainer for the Dale Carnegie System for several years before developing her own method.

Her clients include some of the largest companies in the world; she has trained countless professionals, in person and via online courses, to take charge of their life. She has volunteered as a trainer for www.solidaritynow.org (a humanitarian organization supported by UNHCR).She is on the board of advisors for the main magazine on Modern Stoicism: THE STOIC, and is co-organizer of 2019 STOICON (Annual meeting of Stoics worldwide). Founding member of The Stoic Society of Athens (Hosted at www.agiorgiti-residence.com).

Dr. Alkistis Agio is the author of several books:

- *Thalassa, The Spirit of The Mediterranean* (Self published)
- *You Can Realize Your Dreams* (Cosmos Publishers New York)
- *The Answer is Within* (Kedros Publishers)
- *Greece's Secret Energy Gates* (Kedros Publishers)
- *Happiness Now* (Fereniki Publishers)
- *Euphoria* (Amazon)
- *From Fear To Freedom. (Amazon)*